A doctor reflects on the t

The Shepherd is my Lord

Janet Goodall

James Goodall

May He lead you, too.

CMF
Christian Medical Fellowship

The Shepherd is my Lord
A doctor reflects on the twenty-third psalm

© 2007 Janet Goodall

Published by Christian Medical Fellowship,
157 Waterloo Road, London, England SE1 8XN
www.cmf.org.uk

Cover design by S2 Design and Advertising

ISBN: 978 0 906747 37 7

Body typeset in Palatino 9.75/12

Printed in Great Britain by Stanley L Hunt (printers) Ltd,
Midland Road, Rushden, Northants

Contents

Dedication		*ii*
Acknowledgements		*ii*
Foreword		*iii*
Psalm 23		*v*
Introduction		*vi*
1	Lord – and Shepherd	*1*
2	I am the Good Shepherd	*5*
3	The Lord is *my* Shepherd	*9*
4	The Lord is *our* Shepherd	*14*
5	I shall not be in want	*20*
6	Green pastures and quiet waters	*25*
7	He restores my soul	*30*
8	Restoration and transformation	*35*
9	He leads…He guides in paths of righteousness	*40*
10	He leads…He guides *me*	*47*
11	Walking *together* through the valley of the shadow of death	*55*
12	Your rod and your staff, they comfort me	*60*
13	You prepare a table before me in the presence of my enemies	*67*
14	You anoint my head with oil	*75*
15	My cup overflows	*84*
16	Goodness and mercy will follow me….	*92*
17	…all the days of my life	*98*
18	I shall dwell in the house of the Lord….	*108*
19	In the house of the Lord – for ever?	*117*
20	Love bids us welcome	*127*
21	I know my sheep and my sheep know me	*139*

Dedication

These musings are gratefully offered back to the Shepherd who inspired them. Under him, they come with love and thanks to my old boss, now friend for half a century, Peggy Edmunds.

Acknowledgements

I am grateful to Peter Saunders and the staff of the Christian Medical Fellowship, especially the Publications Committee under Allister Vale's chairmanship, for agreeing to publish this little volume. Bob Carling and Rachael Pickering have worked hard as under-shepherds in keeping a watchful eye on the manuscript and bringing into line any textual waywardness. I am very grateful for their patience and competence, as well as for so kindly including me in so many of the editorial discussions and decisions.

Graham Cotton and Astrit Rrukaj deserve a big thank you for coming to my rescue with their computing skills. The photograph on the back cover was taken by Marit Torkildsen and I thank her. Also, thank you to the families who have agreed to my using their personal stories. Simon Fitter, deputy head verger of Gloucester Cathedral, kindly checked the quotation used in chapter 17, and I am grateful to him for that. Valerie MacKay encouraged me to consider further the views expressed by her husband Professor Donald MacKay as set out in chapter 19, and for this I thank her.

Two clergy friends have read all or part of the manuscript and I am grateful. Having said this though, I am entirely responsible for what I have said in this book, based on my understanding of Scripture.

Grateful acknowledgements are made to the following publishers:

Ambassador Press for permission to quote from the book by Andrew Murray on page 48.

Inter-Varsity Press (IVP) for permission to quote from the books by John Stott on pages 17, 72 and 73.

Send the Light Ltd for permission to quote from the book by AW Tozer on pages 88 and 89.

Solway Publications for permission to quote from the book by Gareth Jones on pages 17 and 18.

SPCK for permission to quote from the books by Tom Wright on pages 101 and 120.

The Canterbury Press for permission to quote from the book by A Ryrie on page 48.

The MacMillan Press for permission to quote from the book by W Temple on page 72.

Foreword

I first met Janet Goodall when I was a medical student, and ever since then she has been an inspirational role model as a gifted and innovative paediatrician and as a gentle and caring Christian servant. In this unique book she reflects on the message and wisdom of the twenty-third psalm. These well known words are illuminated with fresh insights from biblical research, woven together with personal reflections.

Janet's character is embedded in this book. Her lifelong habit of applying detailed knowledge of Scripture to everyday life and situations is spread across the pages. Intermingled with this wisdom are fascinating stories from her career in paediatrics, alongside tales gleaned from her myriad life experiences and travels. This is not Bible study in the usual sense but a demonstration of the way in which the Word of God has been lived out in Janet's experience over 50 years, informing, leading and nourishing.

Each chapter reverberates with reflections from her life – the paradoxical richness of a life spent in caring for the weak and disabled. There are stories from her clinical practice in Britain, Uganda, Albania and elsewhere across the globe. But Janet is not living in a nostalgic past. She has always been concerned to integrate her faith with the challenges of modern life. In this book she grapples in a fresh way with the contemporary problems of bioethics and society as they impact practically on her life as a doctor.

There is a wonderful honesty and sanity in Janet's writing. There are no easy answers or slick solutions to the painful realities of caring for dying or abused children. Janet does not sanitise or minimise the suffering she has witnessed, or the uncertainties and perplexities of a life of faithful Christian discipleship. Yet her writing is penetrated with the faith, hope and love that come from her experience of following the Chief Shepherd. It's a remarkable paradox that someone who has witnessed so much inexplicable suffering, and cared for so many children as they slipped from life to death, still has such a keen and practical appreciation of the future hope of the resurrection.

Now in her seventies, Janet continues to be an international ambassador for Christ. My prayer is that this book will take her special insights and profound experience to a wider audience. It is a delight to read and I commend it to you.

John Wyatt
Professor of Neonatal Paediatrics
University College Hospital, London

Psalm 23

A psalm of David

[1] *The LORD is my shepherd, I shall not be in want.*

[2] *He makes me lie down in green pastures,*
he leads me beside quiet waters,

[3] *he restores my soul.*
He guides me in paths of righteousness
for his name's sake.

[4] *Even though I walk*
through the valley of the shadow of death,
I will fear no evil,
for you are with me;
your rod and your staff,
they comfort me.

[5] *You prepare a table before me*
in the presence of my enemies.
You anoint my head with oil;
my cup overflows.

[6] *Surely goodness and love will follow me*
all the days of my life,
and I will dwell in the house of the LORD for ever.

Introduction

> *We are his people, the sheep of his pasture.*
> *(Psalm 100:3)*

On hearing that I was proposing to make this study, a friend warned me about the dangers of anthropomorphism, attributing human personality traits to animals. This verse encourages us to look in the opposite direction and detect ovine characteristics amongst the people of God. I hope that I have not overdone the analogy, but sheep and humans have more in common with each other than might at first be supposed, at least in terms of the life of the spirit.

In his classic book *A Shepherd's Life*, written almost a century ago about Wiltshire shepherds, WH Hudson comments: '...these old Bible stories have a reality and significance for the shepherd of the down country which they have lost for modern minds'.[1] This is still sadly true of whole societies, even where sheep and grass abound. Despite being sung so often at weddings and funerals, there must be those for whom Psalm 23 lacks full meaning.

Many city dwellers might never have seen a sheep in the flesh, and the lamb section of the supermarket scarcely conveys the right image. Those from poorer parts of the world might look with interest at pictures torn from a magazine, perhaps brightening the walls of a classroom or hut. In the supposedly developed world, although fascinated by televised sheepdog trials, relatively few of us are likely to have observed the daily life of a real live shepherd. In any case, there are big differences between the lives of today's western shepherds and those of David's day. Inhabitants of icebound territories, barren deserts or fishing communities will have even dimmer ideas about sheep and shepherding. Bible translators in the frozen north of Canada (where people knew neither sheep nor grass) began their version of the twenty-third psalm with 'The Lord is my walrus-keeper!'

Psalm 23 is timeless in its application, being old yet ever new. It has become my life psalm, each verse applying to various stages of my journey, so I am always glad to learn more about it. This quest has been enriched by reading Phillip Keller's *The Shepherd Trilogy*[2] and Nogah Hareuveni's *Desert and Shepherd in Our Biblical Heritage*.[3] Even though times have changed, David would have enjoyed browsing through these! For years Keller earned his living on a sheep ranch so became well qualified to share his observations with us. Hareuveni, an experienced Jewish explorer and writer, describes Israel's nature and landscape as a backdrop to an improved understanding of the Bible, and relates this to his study of Psalm 23 in particular.

Some of the material presented here was used previously in a publication that comprised daily readings for doctors, *The Doctor's Life Support*.[4] I am grateful to Professor Alan Johnson for suggesting that those pieces should be expanded into this volume and since then I have had 20 years for further reflection. Alan held office as President of the Christian Medical Fellowship (CMF) and before his untimely death had made time to read and comment on the manuscript. As a son of Douglas Johnson, the founding father of CMF, he shared the same enthusiasm for bringing Christian standards into medical practice, especially for students. Both father and son were noted for their shepherding and many of us, worldwide, must now feel keenly this latest loss of an esteemed and wise friend.

Since student days onwards, CMF has lived up to its title for me, providing not only valuable biblical and ethical teaching but also the friendship of so many other Christians across the world. It is therefore especially satisfying that the Publications Committee has agreed to publish the book and that Professor John Wyatt has kindly contributed the Foreword. Our shared prayer is that it will help others to follow more closely the Lord our Shepherd and perhaps encourage others to find, know and follow him too.

As I was coming to the end of writing, a friend asked how long it had taken me. The answer was 'A lifetime!' I thank God for those who, from my earliest days, have helped to teach, guide and encourage me. As well as my Christian forebears, there are too many to mention individually but, from my third junior doctor post onwards, John and Peggy Edmunds became role models for the practice of godly medical care. I still value Peggy's friendship, and that of so many others who daily reflect the image of our Lord and Shepherd in their costly commitment to caring for diseased, distressed and disadvantaged people across the world.

Each of us will be able to add and apply our own insights as we absorb more of the nourishment on offer in the Shepherd Psalm. This will involve taking time to graze in its pastureland, not merely to gobble (or gabble) our way through it. Just as well digested grass builds up the sheep, so feeding on God's Word will, through his Spirit, prompt a growth spurt for the soul.[5] A healthy appetite for ruminating over the Scriptures is a good indication that we are truly the people of God and the sheep of his pasture.

Regarding the capitalisation of the word shepherd, 'Shepherd' has been used when referring to a member of the Godhead and 'shepherd' in all other cases. Unless otherwise stated, biblical references are from the New International Version.

1 Hudson WH. *A Shepherd's Life*. Fresno, CA: Linden Publishing Co Inc, 2004 (originally published 1910).

2 Keller P. *The Shepherd Trilogy: A Shepherd Looks at the 23rd Psalm, A Shepherd Looks at the Good Shepherd, A Shepherd Looks at the Lamb of God.* Grand Rapids, Michigan: Zondervan, 1996.

3 Hareuveni N (translated by Frenkley H). *Desert and Shepherd in Our Biblical Heritage.* Jerusalem: Neot Kedumim, 1991.

4 Crouch M, Winton R (eds). *The Doctor's Life Support.* London: Christian Medical Fellowship, 1986, 1994.

5 1 Peter 2:2

Lord – and Shepherd

To clarify the meaning of a word, as any crossword addict knows, it can help to look it up in a dictionary. My *Concise Oxford Dictionary* has ten possible uses for the word lord, applying it to a ruler, a peer of the realm, various expletives (when used with a prefix), and to a Lord Chancellor or a bishop. To address someone as 'my lord' indicates respect, whilst to be lordly means either to act with grandeur and magnificence or to convey haughtiness and disdain. What did the title mean to David?

Opposite ends of the scale

In some editions of the Bible, when the word LORD appears in the Old Testament as a reference to God, it is always printed in capital letters to indicate respect and reverence. Presumably David's use of the title reflects the same humble appreciation of the greatness and authority of his God. Elsewhere he specifically says, 'the Lord is on his heavenly throne'.[1] Yet in the next breath of this first verse of Psalm 23, he also refers to him as 'shepherd', which in human terms is right at the other end of the social scale. In this he had the example of his forefather Israel who, when blessing his grandsons, had referred to 'the God who has been my shepherd all my life to this day', so the simile had honourable usage.[2]

Shepherding was an activity that the youthful David had known well. Later, if not in his day, Middle Eastern shepherds were generally thought of as being amongst the poorest outcasts of society who could get no other job. As the farmer's youngest son he had been more privileged, sent to keep the sheep when the workforce on the farm was reduced by his older brothers going off to join the current war effort. Even so, it had caused some surprise in the family when, produced for inspection as an afterthought by his father, and not even introduced by name, he was immediately recognised by the prophet Samuel as the one God had chosen for higher things.[3] In course of time, he would be elevated from being a humble shepherd in the fields to becoming a king on his throne, addressed by his inferiors as 'My lord the king'.[4] His was a rise from a simple to a sumptuous life. Yet that does not at once throw light on the unlikely juxtaposition of 'Lord' and 'shepherd', especially as David has put them in the reverse order of his own experience.

Even though shepherds themselves were probably not highly educated in David's day, they would have a greater knowledge of sheep than most. I have on my shelves a little book called *An Introduction to Keeping Sheep*, written by Jane Upton and Dennis Soden.[5] They are both very familiar with this subject, and their own care for sheep has made them want to share their practical experience. They advise about nutrition, dosing against worms and germs, the different breeds and their different needs, and other trials and joys of raising a healthy flock. In short, as pronounced on the book's cover, 'the emphasis is on the essential skills and techniques which should be at any shepherd's fingertips'. So although considered humble by many, a shepherd has to have considerable know-how to raise a successful flock. Even so, the concept of a king stooping to become a shepherd still seems rather far-fetched.

Both ends meet

In human experience it is somewhat rare to find an important and clever person who is also outstandingly humble. There are exceptions, and I class my old friend Denis Burkitt amongst them. His story is told in *Fibre Man* and can only be touched on here.[6] For years he described himself as 'a simple bush surgeon' in Uganda, yet he kept his eyes open and mind alert, methodically recording what he then noticed. One of the many citations he later received speaks of 'his astonishing powers of observation and the originality with which he recognised simple things and developed them to make concepts of outstanding significance'. Another refers to him as 'a medical naturalist', for in the approved manner of other naturalists he plotted the incidence of his chosen subjects over their regional, and later national, distribution. He once said that all that was needed to do research in Africa was a piece of paper and a pencil.

Denis Burkitt's first major discovery saved the lives of hundreds of children afflicted by a disfiguring tumour, which became known as Burkitt's lymphoma as he was the first to identify its distribution and to institute effective therapy. His other great achievement was to compare and contrast African and European alimentary input and output, and so to recommend adding bran to our western diet (a recommendation still much appreciated by the Kellogg Company). For these he was eventually granted the high honour of the Fellowship of the Royal Society,* about a dozen prestigious prizes (including the Gold Medal of the British Medical Association) and many honours from international academic bodies. In 1970, the Queen conferred on him Companionship of the Order of Saint Michael and Saint George.

Despite all this, to meet Denis Burkitt was to meet a humble, godly, gracious and lovable Irishman who gave no hint of the prestige he carried. Lauded as a lecturer all over the world, it is said of him that on one occasion, as he entered the auditorium with the rest of the platform party, he was evidently startled by loud applause from the audience – and turned to stand aside to give precedence to the unknown notable he assumed must be following him! The audience had, of course, been honouring him. Yet above his old desk still hangs a framed copy of 1 Corinthians chapter four, verse seven: 'What do you have that you did not receive?'

There is a lovely passage in the prophecy of Isaiah where the two roles of Lord and Shepherd are combined in the one person. In chapter 40, verse 10 we read, 'See, the Sovereign Lord comes with power, and his arm rules for him'. The very next verse goes on to say, 'He tends his flock like a shepherd: He gathers the lambs in his arms and carries them close to his heart'. The outstretched arm that rules with authority is complemented by the ability to reach down and

---

* Denis Burkitt CMG (1911-1993):

> As a practising surgeon he recognised the characteristics of a new syndrome in African children which is now known as Burkitt's lymphoma. By personal investigations throughout the world he demonstrated that the tumour occurred commonly only under specified climatic conditions in Africa and New Guinea and he has subsequently been responsible for investigations into its possible association with virus infections and holo-endemic malaria. He demonstrated the responsiveness of the tumour to chemotherapy and that cure could be achieved by small doses. He has shown that many diseases vary unexpectedly in incidence over short distances and that a wide variety of diseases vary in incidence in the same way between underdeveloped and developed countries. Some of these may be associated with a low roughage diet. His studies have been responsible for renewed world interest in the geographical distribution of cancer and other apparently non-infectious diseases.
> (Citation on admission to become a Fellow of the Royal Society, 1972)

Other citations echo these words, and I am grateful to Mrs Olive Burkitt for letting me see them.

cuddle a lamb. In another psalm, David reports how he had heard 'that you, O God, are strong, and that you, O Lord, are loving'.[7]

Popular ideas about God are polarised because so many people think of him as possessing only one of two aspects: either he is perceived as a stern judge, constantly totting up the score of people's misdemeanours, or he is a soft old Father Christmas whose job is to love everyone and hand out goodies. Instead, Isaiah's picture shows someone who is tough *and* tender. Because our finite minds find it difficult to imagine an omnipotent being who perfectly combines both these qualities, Isaiah's 'See…' has us wondering where to look.

As with many Old Testament prophecies and perplexities, an old adage will point us in the right direction: 'In the Old the New concealed, and in the New the Old revealed'.

So let's see what revelations await us in the New Testament. The first place to look will be the gospellers' account of the Son of God – God incarnate, who said of himself, 'Anyone who has seen me has seen the Father',[8] but also claimed to be 'the good shepherd'.[9] Might we find in him the resolution of our polarised popular images?

1   Psalm 11:4
2   Genesis 48:15
3   1 Samuel 16:6-13
4   2 Samuel 19:26,27
5   Soden D, Upton J. *An Introduction to Keeping Sheep (second edition)*. Preston: Farming Books and Videos Ltd, 2002.
6   Kellock B. *Fibre Man: The Life-story of Dr. Denis Burkitt*. London: HarperCollins, 1985.
7   Psalm 62:11,12
8   John 14:9
9   John 10:11

2

I am the Good Shepherd

There was indeed a tough side to the one sometimes simplistically portrayed as 'gentle Jesus, meek and mild'. He vigorously cleared his Father's house, the Temple, by throwing out the money changers, thus rousing the murderous anger of hostile religious leaders.[1] He addressed the sternest of his recorded words to those practising loveless legalism,[2] thereby exercising the authority affirmed on occasion by his Father's voice from heaven.[3] He performed amazing miracles of healing and repeatedly showed his power over the natural world – but only a few addressed him as 'Lord', apart from those who truly believed that he was God incarnate.[4]

Although throughout his life Jesus was known to be a descendant of King David, he spelt out his lordship to his disciples only shortly before his death and then, paradoxically, just after he had humbly washed their feet. 'Now that I, your Lord and Teacher, have washed your feet', he said, 'you also ought to wash one another's feet'.[5] In the early church, openly to confess him as Lord, believing that God had raised him from the dead, gave assurance of the speaker's salvation.[6] In days to come, exalted in heaven, he will be proclaimed King of kings and Lord of lords.[7] Yet neither here on earth or as described in heaven does he show any sign of being an arrogant overlord. This same Lord was content to identify himself as 'shepherd' and claimed to be a 'good' one at that.[8] Interestingly, although born to be King, his first visitors were shepherds.

The good and the bad, shepherds and pastors
A shepherd's reputation rests on the way he cares for his flock, and like the shepherd of the Isaiah prophecy, Jesus tenderly took little children – 'the lambs' – into his arms and blessed them.[9] Two of the epistles honour the normally humble role of shepherd by referring to

him as 'that great Shepherd'[10] and even 'the Chief Shepherd'.[11] What is there about a shepherd, then, that fits what we know of Jesus?

Speaking of himself as the 'good' shepherd, our Lord clearly made a distinction between his own care for his flock and the way that bad shepherds are marked by their lack of concern. I once saw a flock of sheep and lambs in a low lying field where almost half of them were limping along, evidently in pain, and I asked who owned them. 'Oh, he's a very bad shepherd', I was told, 'He never comes near his sheep'. Instead of guiding them away from their boggy pasture to safer ground and attending to their infected hooves, he had literally left them to rot. It would not have been so with a good shepherd who, ever vigilant, would have made regular inspection of the sheep and dealt with the first sign of such trouble. It is in similar ways that our Shepherd knows his sheep and cares about them.

Another use of the word shepherd is for the pastor of a religious congregation. Jesus' claim to be a good shepherd was made to a mixed assembly of Jews, but he was speaking as their pastor when he addressed his disciples saying, 'Do not be afraid, little flock'.[12] They were inside his fold, whereas he longed to draw in the many other sheep still outside and unresponsive to his voice, including some of those who were leading the religious opposition. On another occasion he accused those dominant and domineering men of not practising what they preached, and of loading onto their flocks burdens they would not lift a finger to ease.[13] There are good and bad pastors as well as good and bad shepherds.

There is a vivid description of *bad* pastors back in the Old Testament. The prophet Ezekiel conveys God's denunciation of them, despite their appointment as 'shepherds' for his 'sheep', the people of Israel. He pronounces them to be selfish, lazy, profiteering and careless of the lost, sick and injured sheep he had put in their charge. Instead of tending the sheep, they were acting harshly and brutally towards them so that the flock had become scattered and prey to predators. There are also severe words for the strong sheep amongst the rest as they jostle the weaker ones, trampling their pasture and muddying their drinking water. The bad shepherds and bullying sheep would be dismissed and instead, says the Almighty, he himself would tend the sheep and save those truly his own.[14]

The Good Shepherd

Intriguingly, in verses 23 and 24 of this passage, God promises to appoint over them (*emphasis mine*): 'one shepherd, my servant David, and…he will tend them and be their shepherd. I the Lord will be their God, *and my servant David will be prince among them'*. As there had been an interval of over three centuries between the reign of King David and the coming of the prophet Ezekiel, this reference seems to be looking ahead to someone in David's line, with the same pastoral heart as his. Who better to fulfil this prophecy than the one we now know as the Good Shepherd? We are told that when he saw the crowds he had compassion on them because they were 'harassed and helpless, like sheep without a shepherd'.[15]

So how did Jesus describe his shepherding? In John chapter ten, the picture he gives of a good shepherd is in sharp contrast to the behaviour of the bad ones described by Ezekiel. The good shepherd knows his sheep by name, and they in turn get to know him so well that they will trustingly follow his familiar voice as he leads them out to find new fields and pastures green. Bad shepherds are careless of the sheep's welfare, run away from danger and are only interested in themselves, whereas the good shepherd is willing to face the marauders and even to lay down his life for the sheep. Elsewhere, we have a picture of his leaving 99 sheep together whilst he goes out to search for one that had wandered away and got lost, with general rejoicing when he finds and retrieves it.[16] He cares not only for the flock as a whole but also for the individuals within it – and those who wander away from it.

By these pictures and parables, Jesus was saying that his love was not constrained by self-interest, but was truly and completely self-giving. He showed the fullest extent of his love in his atoning death – when the Good Shepherd was finally crowned king. Yet unlike the crowning of David, the earlier shepherd king, his crown was made of thorns.[17] At the time, it was a mockery of a coronation but one day the nations will assemble before him as, enthroned in heavenly glory, he will exercise judgment over them. He will separate the people from one another 'as a shepherd separates the sheep from the goats'. Once again the images merge. The Shepherd will gather his own flock into his kingdom, commending them for their faithful following, but as the Lord Almighty he will condemn the heartless and heedless because they have failed to show love, either to the needy or to him.[18]

Goats in sheep's clothing?
Western sheep and goats are easily distinguishable, but the Israeli varieties tend to confuse casual observers until they notice that goats have floppier ears and hold their tails aloft whilst sheep's ears are smaller and their tails hang down. In human terms, members

of certain faiths have characteristic customs and clothing, useful in identifying the faithful. They might look alike, but not all have true heart allegiance to their faith. Conversely, professing Christians and non-believers might not always be easily distinguishable externally. What makes the difference is behaviour based on belief. The expert eye of our Shepherd looks not at the outside but on the inside, and he immediately dissociates semblance from sincerity. He knows his own sheep. It is possible to deceive everyone but him. His self-giving love was for all, and he longs for us all to reciprocate by a heartfelt response of loving and obedient commitment to him, combined with a deep concern for others to know him, too.

When I was eight months old my godly grandfather, sharing this concern but anticipating my ability to read by several years, gave me a little book of true stories about the faith of children. He was dead by the time I got beyond the pretty picture on the cover: snow bound sheep and lambs looking expectantly towards their shepherd and his dog, toiling towards them up a wintry slope. I still have that book, *The Good Shepherd and his lambs.*[19] Its author hoped that the book would 'lead youthful hearts to Jesus the Good Shepherd'. In time, as was no doubt my grandfather's prayer, it was the image of the devoted Shepherd that drew my own young heart to him.

1   Luke 19:45-48
2   Matthew 23:13-29
3   Matthew 3:17
4   John 6:68, 9:35-38
5   John 13:14
6   Romans 10:9
7   Revelation 19:16
8   John 10:11,14
9   Mark 10:16
10 Hebrews 13:20
11 1 Peter 5:4
12 Luke 12:32
13 Matthew 23:2-4
14 Ezekiel 34:1-31
15 Matthew 9:36
16 Luke 15:3-7
17 Matthew 27:29
18 Matthew 25:31-33,41-46
19 Witherby HF. *The Good Shepherd and his lambs*. London and Glasgow: Pickering and Inglis, undated.

3

The Lord is *my* Shepherd

My family's Easter holidays were usually spent in the English Lake District, where I was captivated by the story of a local shepherd who had gone after his lost sheep in thick snow and died in a snowdrift. That story, together with the picture on the cover of Grandpa's little book, and what I'd been taught about the Good Shepherd himself, all blended into the image of someone who cared enough to give his life to save and to keep me close, like one of his little lambs. The image sharpened when the Sunday School I attended gave Psalm 23 as the Bible passage that the children were to learn by heart during the week.

After all these years, I well remember standing in our kitchen and repeating the psalm's six verses with my mother as audience. After the recital, she asked me two simple questions: 'Is the Lord really *your* Shepherd?' and 'Have you ever asked him to be?' I feel confident now that whether consciously invited or not, the one who had taken little children up into his arms and blessed them already had me in his care. However, it was a memorable milestone on my journey when my mother and I went up to kneel by my bed and thanked him for his self-giving love, asking him to be *my* shepherd for the rest of my life. That he has been, and Psalm 23 has always been special, never hackneyed, to me.

The Good Shepherd offers his life for the sheep

There is now much debate in theological circles about the doctrine of substitutionary atonement: 'How could a God of love punish his own Son for sins he had not committed? This is not the only message of the cross, but it is a biblical one.[1] Although the phrase was not in my childish vocabulary, the concept of Jesus taking our punishment was one that I could have grasped when quite small, thanks to the intervention of my beloved big brother.

There had been a shameful occasion when, in the grip of bad temper, I had snatched up a small hard brush and hit him. 'Hold out your hand', said my concerned mother, no doubt reluctantly about to carry out a modified version of doing to me as I had done to him. 'No, Mummy', said George, 'Don't hit her! Hit me again instead'. This offer at once filled me with remorse, repentance and a new surge of affection for him. I knew that our mother loved us both but I did not wait to see whether sentence was carried out or not because, like Peter after denying his Lord, I had gone out and wept bitterly.

There was no such reprieve for the Son of God, for he and the Father had agreed that he should pay the penalty our sins deserved. On a smaller scale, my brother's love for me had made him volunteer to take my punishment, so drawing from me both contrition and renewed devotion. The divine plan was for the Son's loving sacrifice to remove our guilt by our repentance and his forgiveness, so restoring the relationship with God that we had been designed for. Our mother was no doubt grieved by my behaviour, but would have found it hard to do to George what I had done to him. We often forget that simply because Father and Son were one, the sacrifice was made by them *both*, and they both loved the whole world enough to go through with it.

Broken relationships can only be repaired by love

That God so loved the world is such potentially life-changing good news and in my work as a paediatrician I met so many families who needed their lives to be changed by his sacrificial love.[2] I recall an infant who was brought in nearly dead with a fractured skull and other injuries, both new and old. His pretty little mother was, after a fashion, a poetess and had married a big, strong and approachable enough man, his arms heavily tattooed. He was clearly fond of the child, but produced no explanation as to what could have happened. At that time I was feeling strongly that punitive action towards many supposedly abusive parents did not correct their behaviour, which was so often based on ignorance more than malice. The trend at the time was for relationships, however faulty, to be torn apart and the child sent into care instead of serious attempts being made to work with the family unit as a whole. We felt that these couples needed to be taught how to be better parents, their child still with them, and ideally these families should all be housed together for a time in a caring (preferably prayerful) environment.

When the little boy had recovered from his physical injuries, we therefore transferred the threesome hundreds of miles away to the only unit to be found at that time where this philosophy was shared. After an interval I went to visit them. The child's injuries remained unexplained, although the chief suspect was still the father. The accommodation was rather cramped and as the family sat on the bed I found myself kneeling in front of them, where I was close enough to observe that one of the father's tattoos was a cross. I forget now how the conversation went, but I pointed to the cross and reminded them what it stood for. Their response (and my posture) made it natural to pray with them.

As soon as the prayer ended, the father confessed to having hurt his little son, 'When I hit his head against the wall, I was remembering what my Dad had done to me'. The sins of the fathers *are* visited on their children but there is still power in the cross of Christ to cancel out that legacy. I wish that the story had a happy ending, but despite the father's confession and contrition, his poetess divorced him. Their child recovered well – and even as I write I follow them with my prayers. They remain part of the world that God so loved.

Such love

One Good Friday, still a child, I was sitting high up on a sunny Lakeland hillside within sight and sound of a rippling peat-stained beck, looking out over hundreds of scattered sheep grazing on the slopes below me. Ignorant of Israeli timekeeping, I was waiting for the church clock in the valley to strike what I thought had been the hour of crucifixion in Jerusalem. The Lord, creator of all this beauty, had been willing to pay such a terrible price to draw into his fold those who were wandering like straying sheep.[3] The Good Shepherd had given his life for the sheep – yet with a statement over his head proclaiming him to be Jesus, the King of the Jews.[4] Most watchers by the cross did not realise that they were witnessing the greatest act of love possible from their Lord and Shepherd, combined in the one unique person. Yet, like the domineering sheep portrayed by Ezekiel, and despite thinking that they were chosen members of God's flock, they could not like David (and now me) say, 'The Lord is *my* shepherd'. They had not listened to his voice or followed him, and were still outside the fold.

One of my women friends gets very cross should her husband refer to her (even in jest) as 'the wife'. She wants him to acknowledge her as '*my* wife' or, better still, to use her name. They have a special relationship because of their mutual commitment. So it is with our

Lord and Shepherd who knows each of us by name. Yes, he has grandeur and authority and his Word should be our command, but he also has the concern and compassion of a shepherd for our well being, even when we are in troubles of our own making. He says, 'Come to me, all you who are weary and burdened, and I will give you rest…For my yoke is easy and my burden is light'.[5]

The easy yoke

No doubt the analogy Jesus was making there concerned the yoke used in those days to link together a pair of oxen for the hard task of dragging a simple plough through the notoriously stone strewn fields. To visit Israel and see all those stones gives a lot of insight into his parable of the sower, for these cannot be the easiest fields to plough before sowing. Two yoked oxen would make the job easier than one working alone, especially if the yoke were comfortable and smoothly honed, like those undoubtedly fashioned at the carpenter's shop in Nazareth. Perhaps Jesus' thoughts were on his past handiwork when he referred to 'my' yoke being easy.

The only yoke I have seen on a sheep was in the beautifully remote Shetland Isles, for years famous for woollen knitwear. A sheep disposed to fight or bully others is put in a neck yoke – a cumbersome wooden frame that effectively stops any violent head-butting. Others, prone to stray, might push their way through thorn bushes and hedges, tearing off their valuable wool as they do so. The neck yoke controls them too. This is not the easy yoke Jesus was referring to, for it restrains more than relieves and, although protective, is an extra burden rather than being 'light'. For us to accept our Lord's invitation to put on his metaphorical yoke is not to find ourselves restricted, as with a neck yoke, but full of gratitude for his lightening of our load. Like Paul, we might share our yoke with fellow workers or, unlike him, with a partner for life. Paul also found when particularly hard pressed that the Lord provided his own great strength and all-sufficient grace to overcome Paul's weakness for the task.[6] Just as the shepherd carries the lambs and is gentle with the pregnant ewes, so our Lord takes the strain.

Commitment to him as Lord acknowledges his sovereignty over our lives, but commitment to him as Shepherd finds this to be a loving rule, designed to give us the best of lives because lived under his wise direction and enabled with his strength. We love him because he first loved us, and love is the fulfilment of the law, for if we love someone we want to do what we can to please the beloved.[7] After he had washed the disciples' feet, their Lord taught them that love and obedience are intertwined.[8] He also emphasised that they were to love each other with the same self-giving love as his own, expressed in voluntary servanthood, not reluctant servility.[9]

The International Christian Medical and Dental Association, as its name implies, is a worldwide fellowship of Christians in the two health care professions of medicine and dentistry. Members are encouraged, by regional and international conferences and by relevant literature, to behave and to think in a Christian manner, taking their Lord and Shepherd as mentor and guide. They are reminded of his example by the Association's logo of a cross, with a bowl and towel before it. The emblem signifies their intention to practise their professions in the same spirit of sacrificial love and service as that shown by their Lord. Their training might have given them a certain authority, but it is to be used with humility, just as his was.

1   Hebrews 9:11-28; McGrath A. *Making sense of the cross*. Leicester: Inter-Varsity Press, 1994; Wright NT. *Evil and the justice of God*. London: SPCK, 2006.

2   John 3:16

3   Isaiah 53:6

4   Matthew 27:37

5   Matthew 11:28-30

6   2 Corinthians 12:9

7   Romans 13:10; 1 John 4:19-21

8   John 15:9,10

9   John 13:12-17

4

The Lord is *our* Shepherd

By definition, a flock is made up of more than one sheep. As everyone who loves and follows Jesus can claim that 'the Lord is *my* Shepherd', so each member of his flock can also say that he is '*our* Shepherd'. By underlining the need for mutual love amongst all who own him as Shepherd, our Lord longed for the same loving unity between them all as he knew with his Father. Some Christian communities maintain this vision and, in obedience to his teaching, reckon that love for him and for each other are priorities in their rule of life. For them, subdivisions on denominational or other grounds are of only secondary importance – differences to be lived with. To our shame, not all members of his flock follow this pattern.

It is a favourite expression amongst shepherds that 'a sheep's worst enemy is another sheep'. Because of their close proximity, one sheep can pass on infectious disease to another as heads butt together, or they establish a pattern of behaviour that is all too readily copied and carried on by their young. It is sad when these hazards also affect members of the Good Shepherd's flock. Instead of presenting an impressively united front, subdivisions can become of primary importance and partisanship ever more strident. The outsider's view of the church is coloured by any obvious disharmony amongst those who claim to own Christ as their Lord. Instead of wanting to follow him themselves, as had been his prayer for those still outside his fold,[1] unbelievers make mock of such infighting.

United we stand, but....

We must all be familiar with the infantile behaviour which says, 'That's *mine*', or 'I'm not going to be friends with you any more', whether the dispute is over a toy or a territory, or simply the megalomania of a tyrant. We are unhappily accustomed to seeing this acted out in many parts of our war-torn world. Sadly, when Christians disagree, similar confrontations can arise. Even a pastor can turn dictator. Love goes out of the window as sectarianism raises iron curtains between the different members of the body of Christ. Screened off from each other, each is prone to claim unique insights and to keep out of communion those who do not share them. 'That's *my* view, *my* interpretation, and yours is so wrong that I even doubt whether you are a Christian.' This is not fanciful – such things have been said in my presence.

Principles or prejudices?

Even amongst sincere Christians, 'acting on principle' can really be acting out prejudice. Maintaining ideals, whilst showing love to those who think differently, requires the kindness and patience of the Spirit to ease the process of reconciliation. Each party needs prayerfully to meet and listen to the other as, together with their leaders, they try to sort out essentials of faith and conduct from subsidiary matters. Any agreement to differ must avoid generating hostile factions, remembering the prayer of our Lord Jesus that we all might be one in him. Instead it seems to be so much easier for discussants to be on the defensive, widening instead of bridging the gap between them.

In my youth, the labels orthodox and liberal, or 'evangelicals and the rest', were attached to those practising what are much less uncontroversial matters for many, if not most, western Christians. Sadly, some of the old taboos have been exported and in some places have almost become doctrinal issues. Reading works of fiction, going to a theatre or cinema, wearing makeup or stylish clothing, adopting a smart hairstyle, dancing or taking part in amateur theatricals – to name but a few – these were activities likely to have participants labelled as wordly and so out of bounds for the faithful. Other people might still be judged as being 'one of us' by what they allowed or disallow, but today such shibboleths are more likely to be about church music or forms of service, the use of charismatic gifts, or who is or is not allowed into church membership and leadership. Yet the graceless barricades still go up, sometimes in even pettier ways.

Cliques made up of the like-minded splinter church fellowships and even the correspondence columns of Christian magazines can be spattered with sarcasm or worse. In his book *What's So Amazing About Grace?* Philip Yancey goes into this in greater depth; it is well worth consulting.[2]

The origin of the word shibboleth may now be forgotten. It arose after the men of Ephraim felt left out when the men of Gilead went to war without asking for their help. Feeling snubbed, the Ephraimites refused to accept the explanation offered, namely that there had been a breakdown in communication. (There is nothing new!) Instead they attacked the Gileadites, lost the battle and fled back towards home, but as they tried to cross the river Jordan they were challenged by the men of Gilead. Just as most English people find it hard to roll the 'r' when speaking French, the Gileadites knew that Ephraimites always pronounced shibboleth as 'sibboleth'. This therefore became a test word to identify those on the opposite side, who were then promptly slaughtered. This could all have been avoided if both sides had not leapt to mistaken conclusions in the first place.[3] There are lessons for us here about being gracious in listening to one another rather than being so quick to judge, destructive criticism at the ready.

Why so much disunity?

The vexed question remains: 'We might expect flak from secular thinkers, but why so much disagreement between Christians?' Providing at least a partial answer are these severe words from James: 'What causes fights and quarrels among you?..You do not have because you do not ask God. When you ask, you do not receive, because you ask with wrong motives, that you may spend what you get on your pleasures'.[4] Prayerlessness and self-interest, says James, are the breaks in the circuit, the bypaths that take us away from righteous paths and persuade us to put up 'No Entry' signs for those who do not know our passwords. It has been rightly said that those who pray together are likely to stay together, but it can be rare for holders of different viewpoints to share a prayer meeting.

Those able and willing to cross boundaries, whether denominational or otherwise, often find that differences are in the expression, not the essentials, of our faith. There remain some who have not been given (or taken) such opportunities. Fierce disputes can still arise over secondary issues, even when both sides truly share the same basic biblical principles but then throw texts, traditions or theories at each other when trying to prove a subsidiary point. Others might find that more than one precept applies and seek to balance, for example, justice with mercy. It simply pushes the other party further into the opposite corner to cry 'Legalist!' to those majoring on justice, or 'Liberal!' to those who favour mercy.

Lovers of formal church services can decry and even sneer at the more relaxed, and vice versa. Supposedly based on being one flock following one Shepherd, the intended unity breaks down without the willingness on both sides for attentive listening, repentance, mutual forgiveness and reconciliation, or at least an agreement to differ amicably. This does not mean that the minority must meekly allow themselves to be trampled on, their voices silenced by the bleating and butting of the majority. That would be an artificial settlement. On the contrary, unity is not uniformity, and respect by each party for the other's Christian integrity must replace hostility and suspicion if Christ is to be honoured.

As John Stott wrote in *The Message of Ephesians*: 'We need to get the failures of the church on our conscience, to feel the offence to Christ and the world which these failures are, to weep over the credibility gap between the church's talk and the church's walk, to repent of our readiness to excuse and even condone our failures, and to determine to do something about it. I wonder if anything is more urgent today, for the honour of Christ and the spread of the gospel, than that the church should be, and should be seen to be, what by God's purpose and Christ's achievement it already is…a family of reconciled brothers and sisters who love their Father and love each other, the evident dwelling place of God by his Spirit. Only then will the world believe in Christ the Peacemaker. Only then will God receive the glory due to his name'.[5]

When challenged as to what he considered the greatest commandment, Jesus cited two: to have an all-encompassing love for God, and to love a neighbour as much as you love yourself. All other 'laws' must be subservient to these.[6] When Christians disagree, remembering his teaching should instigate humility and prayerfulness first, then serious discussion, mutual attentiveness and godly debate. All this will involve both meeting and listening to each other instead of writing angry letters from afar or shooting off reflex e-mails, which of course tend to be coloured by the reader's frame of mind as well as the writer's choice of words. The nub of the problem can be a stubborn intransigence that rejects conciliatory invitations and prefers to keep its distance. This often arises over matters on which the Bible offers principles, yes, but no obvious directions about how to practise them in specific circumstances.

All one body we

After being the target of such flak from fellow Christians near and far, Gareth Jones wrote the book *Coping with Controversy*.[7] In it he said: 'The unity of Christ's body should constitute the prime impetus to resolution of conflict between Christians…We have to learn how to live with one another in love, and also how to disagree with one another in love…Sometimes we will be wrong and have to admit that we are wrong. But even if convinced that we are correct, we may still have a great deal to learn from our adversaries and we will recognise our constant need of each other in the body of Christ'.

As a medical doctor, the author knew that the human body has certain parts, such as muscles, whose actions can be in direct opposition to those of others. Yet it is with tensile strength that they keep the whole mechanism healthily balanced as long as the pathway from the brain is working well. Similarly, members of the body of Christ have uniquely different personalities, gifts and activities.[8] The human body depends on a good solid backbone to maintain an upright position, but also needs sensitive, flexible fingers and even fluttering eyelashes to fulfil all its functions effectively. The members of Christ's body need to accept each others' different roles, integrated into a complete and effective whole and ready to do what he has assigned for them to do.[9] Our Lord's aim is for each to work together to the good of the whole, attaining maturity by learning to speak the truth in love, and all under the headship of Christ, who is the ultimate nerve centre of the body.[10] Only his Spirit, whose first fruit is love, can enable this to happen.

Interdependence

Our Shepherd knows his own sheep by name and might call some to explore unmapped territory instead of following ancient well-worn tracks – indeed in matters of ethics, new territory is opening up all the time. The pioneers need to listen hard to be sure it really is his voice calling and that this is not just an ego trip – a tendency to proud independence and going it alone, or even a bid for fame. That excluded, they are still part of the one flock, following the Shepherd if not always the herd.

Just as it is possible to make the mistake of confusing outward conformity with heart allegiance, so it is easy to treat as outsiders those whose hearts are responsive to the Lord's leading but whose work (and perhaps appearance) is out of the ordinary run. Those whose lot is in greener pastures should resist the traps implicit in a critical spirit and the cliquishness that cold-shoulders the nonconforming. Instead there is special need to cultivate prayerful partnership with those who have obeyed the call to follow rougher or more hazardous tracks. This can apply to those with an offbeat mission, whether at home or abroad, who have returned to the sending church and been both saddened and gladdened to realise how much a congregation has truly engaged with them in understanding prayer. To be asked, 'Have you had a good trip?' or 'See now, which country was it you went to?' does not inspire a sense of being a viable part of that body of believers.

Face-value judgment can kill

Anyone who has studied the mental processes of little children will
know how for years they judge by appearances, for example mistaking
pills for sweeties, or the fluid in the pretty green bottle with a red label
for a nice drink. The consequences of such mistakes are poisonous.
So are the errors of judgment that label people as 'others' when they,
too, are members of the body of Christ.

As we shall see in chapter 17, it takes years of experience
and instruction before children learn to look ahead and anticipate
the results of their actions. No wonder Paul urged the Ephesian
believers to *grow up*, to take the long view and hold together, building
themselves up in love. This is still a message for all who are seriously
involved in today's controversial issues. The Lord is *our* Shepherd,
and his desire is that we keep the unity of his Spirit through the bond
of peace[11]– that is to pull together under his easy yoke.

1 John 17:20,21
2 Yancey P. *What's So Amazing About Grace?* Grand Rapids, Michigan: Zondervan Publishing House, 1997.
3 Judges 12:1-6
4 James 4:1-3
5 Stott J. *The Message of Ephesians.* Leicester: Inter-Varsity Press, 1991.
6 Matthew 22:35-40
7 Jones G. *Coping with Controversy: Helping Christians Handle Their Differences.* Milton Keynes: Paternoster Press, 1996.
8 1 Corinthians 12:4-12
9 1 Corinthians 12:12-27
10 Ephesians 4:11-16
11 Ephesians 4:3

5

I shall not be in want

In the version of the twenty-third psalm I learned as a child, this phrase read, 'I shall not want'. For young and old alike it would be easy to imply from this that we can have all that we wish for. 'I shall not be in want' puts a different slant on the meaning. A small child, repeatedly rebuked for saying 'I want', learned to change her plea to 'I *need* a biscuit'. She then had to learn that not only are wants not the same as needs but what we might think of as needs are not all essentials. Yet a slogan of a few years ago invited us to 'take the waiting out of wanting'. Many of us can do just that, aided by cash machines, microwave ovens, mobile phones and other forms of push button technology, all designed to give us instant access to whatever it is we desire so urgently.

Episodes of armed robbery are being recorded more and more in Britain and elsewhere. Thieves want goods or cash, often hold people to ransom to get it and, unless traced, hope to want for nothing more for years – nothing, that is, except peace of mind. Even if their hardened consciences no longer trouble them, there is no assurance that they will not eventually land up in jail.

Needs supplied

Some years ago a friend and I were in Uganda and visited a number of grandmothers, caring for up to twelve grandchildren each, the parents having died of AIDS. Not only had these elderly ladies been bereaved of their own sons and daughters but also, at a time of life when they might have expected to be taken care of themselves, they were working hard to care for bereft children of no more than school age. I recall Erivida who lived in a mud hut without running water, light or adequate space for all her grandchildren. She mimed for me how she regularly had to go out to dig and delve to grow their food, how she often got very tired in the process and was usually left feeling hungry herself. Then her face lit up with a wonderful smile, and I was told that she had said, 'But praise God! He is great, he is good. He knows'. We were so moved and left a few shillings to be distributed amongst the grannies by our hostess after we had left. Months later came a message of thanks: 'How did they know we needed anything?' We were even more humbled.

Similarly, when visiting Albania in 1991 as the country opened up to the outside world, two of us were shocked at the degree of poverty we met in a European country. A new local friend, Sergei, invited us to share a meal with him. He had caught a fish and hoarded a bottle of wine and, as we sat at his table, he looked round at us and, beaming with satisfaction, said in all seriousness, 'I am a very rich man'.

Neither Erivida nor Sergei reckoned wealth in material terms. Pressing as their material poverty was, given the love of God along with neighbour love, they were not hankering after more than the basics.

The Good Shepherd knows best

When David added 'I shall not be in want' to the awareness of the Lord being his Shepherd, he was possibly recalling how much he had cared about his own sheep, so could trust that his almighty, shepherding Lord would care even more for him. He must at times have seen the conflict between his plans for the flock and a wayward sheep's desire to head off for what looked like greener grass, only to find itself up to its neck in a swamp, or caught in a thorny thicket. We, too, can be seduced by something that looks desirable but is not our Shepherd's choice for us and will only cause trouble.

Others of David's sheep might have tried to back off the difficult, stony path along which he was taking them, but which he knew was the way to verdant pastureland. In the same way, we can try to disobey our Shepherd's leading, put off by a track that looks too hard. Instead, kicking against his directions, we might search for a short cut to reach the place or position we imagine was simply made for us. Like Humpty Dumpty, we can then have a great fall. The pursuit of our own way can make us suffer, and can also hurt those we love.

Many a parent knows this as their children abandon childhood faith and get into dubious company, or ruin their health with drugs or drink. After his story of the lost sheep, recorded in Luke chapter 15, Jesus told the story of one such headstrong son who demanded a premature inheritance from his father, then spent it all in riotous living; as the King James version puts it, 'he began to be in want'. If he had stayed within range of his father's loving voice he would have lacked nothing, but he could not wait to be up and away. The waiting is *not* taken out of wanting, because learning to wait on him, trusting and obeying him, is an exercise that God will continue to offer us all our lives long. During that time he might also change our desires, so that laying up treasure on earth becomes less important than enjoying his spiritual gifts, now and for ever. Holding on in obedience makes us exert our faith muscles, slowly strengthening them. Like the usual kind of physiotherapy, it can sometimes be a painful exercise, even if eventually a productive one.

In the Garden of Eden, Eve was persuaded to disobey God because the forbidden fruit she was being tempted to taste *looked* so attractive.[1] The consequences of that disobedience are with us still. We should learn from her experience, if not our own, that appearances are all too often deceptive. To put first the accumulation of wealth, the purchase of a fast car and an impressive mansion, or to seek favours from the rich and powerful, can be real temptations in our secular world. However attractive at first sight, the satisfaction we seek does not lie in them, although the Father might generously give some of them to some of us.[2] The promise to those whose trust is in God still holds, whether affluent or poverty stricken: 'And my God will meet all your needs according to his glorious riches in Christ Jesus'.[3] Those riches are not scattered randomly as pennies from heaven, but come as tokens of his love in many different ways.

Tracing rainbows

We sometimes get lovely surprises as to how, as promised, God meets all our needs. Just last week, after driving round various parts of London, I travelled the 200 miles home by motorway, only to be abruptly stopped in my tracks the very next day when the car's clutch failed. I was alone on a long, deserted stretch of country road – but just opposite the only farmhouse in the area! There I was made welcome, offered the use of a telephone to call for the breakdown van and to let my intended hostess know that I was stranded. Bless her, she came out to sit with me until technical help arrived and we had a rare, uninterrupted hour of catching up in each other's company. A day or two earlier and the breakdown could have occurred at rush hour on London's Waterloo Bridge or on a busy motorway which would have been much harder to deal with for all concerned, such a long way from home. To trace the rainbow through the rain is to be reminded that our God keeps his promises, even (perhaps especially) when the outlook is overcast.

My experience was eased by so readily being able to summon help. Others are not so fortunate, but God's promises are not limited by circumstance or culture. The friend who came to sit with me had for a time joined her daughter, a missionary in Africa. She tells the story of how, at a church celebration, the food had already run out and washing up was in progress when an unexpected company of a dozen hungry young men arrived. Apprehensive of appearing inhospitable, she searched in vain for a few remnants of rice from the feast, but was then both relieved and mystified to find that a big red pot of prepared stew had appeared in the previously denuded kitchen. The late arrivals were Masai who would have scorned rice. They demolished the meat with gusto, and the day was saved – much as had happened when Jesus miraculously supplied the best of wine when supplies ran out at the wedding in Cana of Galilee.[4] On this occasion the miracle worker had been a little old African lady who had quietly slipped in her offering, perhaps thinking it was much too late, but in fact it synchronised with God's perfect timing.

Sometimes God preserves his own followers at times of natural disaster, and sometimes he does not. Many believers lost their lives in the great tsunami of 2004. Yet after the huge earthquake in North East Asia in 2005, the only hospitals left standing very close to the epicentre were two run by Christians, able to call for international resources from fellow believers worldwide. Their dedicated care made a great impact on those of other faiths living around them, allaying much previous hostility as well as saving many lives. A glance at the appropriate map shows the significance of those particular survivors' preservation; they in turn became providers for a largely cut off host of homeless and vulnerable people. We are not always so clearly able to trace his hand at work, but it is always there.

Needs supplied

There was at least one episode in David's life when he must have been left marvelling at the organisation needed to take out the wanting from his waiting. This was when his son Absalom was in revolt against David's kingship and the king's army had become hungry and tired and thirsty. Prayer came so naturally to David that we can be sure he would send out an urgent call to his all-seeing and ever caring Lord. Then an unexpected consignment arrived containing all the provisions they needed – a wonderfully comprehensive list of bedding and bowls, pots and produce, with various high protein and high calorie fast foods to re-energise them.[5] Tracing all the cross references to this story shows that the three main sources of this remarkable aid package lived miles apart from each other and well away from the exhausted army, but not too far to converge on the camp when they had each picked up God's SOS message about David's needs.

These suppliers formed a disparate trio. One, Shobi, came from the town of Rabbah, which alone should have put him at enmity with David, for this was a town that he had vengefully captured and plundered before enslaving its residents. The second donor, Makir, had given a home to the lame Mephibosheth, son of Jonathan, until without warning David had taken him away to treat him like a prince. Whatever the facts of the matter, we are not specifically told that Makir had been rewarded for his pains apart from having one less mouth to feed. The third, Barzillai, was a very rich old man of eighty of whom David was very fond and later tried in vain to take with him to Jerusalem. Yet, curious collaborators as they were, they all responded with overwhelming generosity to a need they could only have guessed at. David and his troops were at the end of their collective tether, and found that God was there to meet all their needs. They were no longer in want.

Perhaps that was when David thought of this stanza for his psalm.

1   Genesis 3:6
2   Matthew 6:33
3   Philippians 4:19
4   John 2:1-11
5   2 Samuel 17:27-29

6

Green pastures
and quiet waters

David spoke of the Lord, his Shepherd, making him lie down in green pastures and leading him beside the quiet waters. As he immediately spoke of the restoration of his soul, perhaps it was through such experiences of tranquillity that his ruffled spirits had often been soothed. Over the years I have stayed in two guesthouses with names reminiscent of these pastures and waters, each of them restful and restorative. Old friends have named their retirement home Green Pastures. There can be no doubt that the idea of enjoying a little peace and quiet lies within the application to us of the psalm's second verse, living in top gear as so many of us do. Yet there is more.

Three Warwickshire shepherds were once asked to say what they saw as the chief tasks of their shepherding.* Without hesitation, they all mentioned the same priorities: to attend to the nourishment of the flock, to keep the sheep clean, to protect them from foxes and other dangers, and to establish desirable breeds. Their remaining task was to make sure that the sheep learned to recognise the shepherd's voice, as their shortsighted, bulging sheep's eyes stop them identifying others, including sheep stealers, who might approach them.

Knowing the Shepherd's voice
To take this last point first, Jesus made a similar comment in his analogy of the shepherd and his flock: '…they will never follow a stranger; in fact they will run away from him, because they do not recognise a stranger's voice'.[1] John remarks that Jesus used this figure of speech to teach his flock the importance of tuning in to him for direction, learning to distinguish his voice from any other, even when their vision was so earthbound or clouded that they could not clearly see

---

* I remain grateful to Nigel Lee, who reported and applied the insights of these shepherds at the Keswick Convention in 2005, the year before he died.

him. Listening to him was vital for safety and security. This teaching is important still.

A healthy diet

David's mention of pastureland and watering places reminds us of the Warwickshire shepherds' first point, about keeping the sheep well nourished. At the most basic level, grass and water are essential to maintain a sheep's nutrition, but not just any old grass or scummy, stagnant pond. As human dietary experts today tell us to eat plenty of fresh green vegetables, so sheep gain essential nutrients from fresh, juicy green grass. A journey through sheep farming country gives ample illustration of the importance of grass to sheep. For mile after mile, near and far, the green fields are dotted with the white woollen bundles that represent a scattered flock, constantly on the move as they graze. Lacking upper incisors, they tear up the grass and can spoil the pasture unless allowed to roam. When at last they have had enough, they lie down, suggestive of David's saying that his Lord and Shepherd made him lie down, fully satisfied.

It was noteworthy that after the slaughter of thousands of animals in the United Kingdom foot and mouth disease epidemic of 2001, once the flocks were up and growing again many more of them were seen lying down than before the cull. The grass was richer having been undisturbed for a while and, with fewer mouths to be fed, the sheep were more quickly satisfied – one good effect of a very bad experience.

Water and life go together

Yet neither man nor beast can survive without water. Human travellers often carry bottles of water with them wherever they go. Eastern shepherds look for pools or cisterns whilst their western counterparts provide clean water troughs for the wandering flock. Everywhere, quiet (not static) waters are essential as turbulent streams frighten the sheep and leave them thirsty. There are, though, countries where serious drought is a recurrent problem with no supply of water at all. We become all too familiar with pictures of starving children and dehydrated, dying herds, reminding us that spiritual food and drink are also basic essentials for the survival of the Good Shepherd's flock.

Just as a runaway sheep might find itself on a bare and rocky hillside, with only dry wisps of heather to eat and a terrifying waterfall the only possible thirst quencher, so to neglect proper spiritual refreshment is to head for a spiritual wilderness. Without it, souls who range free of the Shepherd's guidance will lose vitality and can falter and fall away. The message is to stay close to him, well within the sound of his voice – that is, to live in communion with him. Then, after the relaxation of the green pastures – and even after great tribulation[2] – he will lead us on again to find springs of living water.

Food and drink for the soul

So what does the Chief Shepherd offer as nourishment for the soul? Jesus said, 'I am the bread of life. He who comes to me will never go hungry, and he who believes in me will never be thirsty'.[3] In the discussion following this amazing statement, we have John's record of how Jesus referred to his broken body and shed blood, spoken of by the other gospellers in the context of the last Passover supper he would share with his disciples before his death.[4] He said, 'Whoever eats my flesh and drinks my blood has eternal life, and I will raise him up at the last day'.[5] Mysteriously, he refers here to the life giving nature of his broken body and shed blood, something that we remember in our communion services and will think of again in chapter 13.

These gifts of our Lord and Saviour are too precious ever to be taken for granted, yet in the helter-skelter of daily life we can get so preoccupied and even depressed by our own affairs that we forget to turn to him. We can go through life with a frowning spirit, even calling it the daily grind, when instead we should every day lift up to him faces shining with trust and gratitude. Even in the middle of all his lamentations, the prophet Jeremiah remembered how the Lord's love is new every morning, and how great is his faithfulness. Our hope is in him.[6]

Slow down

Recumbent sheep are often seen to be chewing the cud, and sometimes our Shepherd has to make us lie down, perhaps allowing (though, I believe, not always sending) illness, unemployment or other immobility to free us from our busy lives. This gives more time to feed on him in our hearts, and be thankful. Sheep do not need prompting to eat their daily food, but perhaps a good alarm clock would make more of us find time to ruminate on our Shepherd's teachings – to read, mark, learn and inwardly digest the Scriptures and to communicate with him in prayer before facing the pressures of the day.

We sometimes see elderly and infirm sheep, or those grazing as they go uphill, falling on their knees as they eat. Whether ruminating or kneeling, they offer us further clues to the spiritual truth that as we feed prayerfully on God's Word, so we enjoy ongoing, two way communion with him, whatever our stage of life or the nature of our uphill struggles. Just as a baroque quartet depends on a strong, sustained base line from the keyboard player, so his presence is our divine continuo. He is always there to sustain, strengthen and keep our lives in harmony with him and with each other. His voice speaks most clearly in his written Word, prompting us to listen carefully for anything he seems to emphasise. He is also ever ready to hear us as we pray, whether to express praise and thanks or to seek his help for others as well as for ourselves.[7]

Yet if fatigue, sickness or other adversity overwhelm or dispirit us, and he seems far away, he has his own ways of reassuring us. At such a time I once switched on the bedside radio and stumbled across the sound of harmonious voices, singing a message that went straight to my sore heart:

> *Lean on my ample arm, Oh thou depressed,*
> *And I will bid the storm cease in thy breast.*
> *If thou wilt come to me, thou shalt find rest.*

The hidden spring

We might seem to have strayed from consideration of the universal need for water, but there is a link. Food without fluid is dry. Biblical imagery is so richly varied, but if we consider what Jesus, our Shepherd, said about water we find that he was referring to the Holy Spirit.[8] The Spirit's arrival would follow Jesus' resurrection and departure back to the Father, his self-giving and self-sacrificial work of redemption finished. When his physical presence was removed from their sight, the Spirit of Jesus would come, never to leave his flock to cope alone with thirst unsatisfied. It is the Spirit's nudge that alerts us to take note as we read his written Word and learn to respond to his gentle promptings.

Jesus first mentioned the possibility of a spiritual 'spring of water welling up to eternal life' as a contrast to the visible water of Jacob's well.[9] Though essential for quenching physical thirst, well water has to be taken again and again with the risk of its running dry or getting polluted, but whoever partakes of the water he spoke of need never again experience spiritual drought. The proviso is that believers keep walking in step with the Spirit[10] thereby avoiding any unclean actions and attitudes that would grieve him and besmirch others.[11]

Muddying the waters

As the Warwickshire shepherds would no doubt point out, just as sheep must be kept clean, fed and watered, so must the water supply itself be protected from pollution. One way of doing this, as described in my manual of good sheep management, is to float wooden planks in the water trough to stop frisky lambs jumping in with muddy feet, so risking death by drowning as well as fouling of the water. The young, thoughtless and untutored need special guidance and protection.

In parts of the world where the sturdy planks of reliable Bible teachers are in short supply, leaders can be young and relatively untaught, often with occasional access to, rather than ownership of, a Bible. Immature face value judgment can then do harm as these leaders take literally some of the outmoded customs they find recorded in the Old Testament. I once saw men in long white robes leading some sheep towards a small African church, and was told that the sheep were to be slaughtered as part of 'Christian' worship. The worshippers had not realised that the sacrifices for sin, offered under the Old Covenant, foreshadowed the coming of the Lamb of God whose sacrifice once and for all had done away with the requirements of the old ceremonial law. Their waters were still muddied.

In Ezekiel's passage on shepherds and sheep, the Sovereign Lord is not addressing errant lambs but questioning the big bullies of the flock: 'Must my flock feed on what you have trampled and drink what you have muddied with your feet?'[12] One spot of mud in a glass of water clouds it all. Walking through a bog splashes mud onto the walker, and mud sticks. Something must be done about it.

1   John 10:5
2   Revelation 7:13-17
3   John 6:35
4   Luke 22:14-20; John 6:51-58
5   John 6:54
6   Lamentations 3:22-24
7   Philippians 4:4-7
8   John 7:38,39
9   John 4:13-14
10 Galatians 5:25
11 Ephesians 4:29-32
12 Ezekiel 34:18,19

7

He restores my soul

The thought of restoration implies bringing something, or someone, back to a proper state. Muddy sheep can be washed by the rain and made clean again. A grimy art treasure can be restored to its original glory by an expert, or a cache of stolen jewels restored to the rightful owner. Medical skill can revive people about to perish and later send them home, doubly restored. After feeling worn out, we might speak of being restored by taking a shower, a cup of coffee, or a day in green pastures beside still waters. In line with these physical and emotional forms of renewal, we need to know what has gone wrong with the soul that it, too, should need restoration. Is it lost, almost dying, or just jaded and faded and in need of an expert's touch?

There is certainly no need for souls to stay out in the cold, for Jesus said that he had come to seek and to save what was lost.[1] He also said that it was possible to perish, but that 'whoever' believes and trusts in his sacrificial self-giving love will instead receive eternal life.[2] What about a lacklustre soul, or one that has got soiled? Mud has done its dirty work on one who, even so, is still assuredly part of the flock. Although ewes lick their newborn lambs, they cannot lick themselves clean as cats and dogs do, and neither can our souls cleanse themselves. We need to echo David's anguished cry in that other great psalm of his, written after he had erred from God's ways like a lost sheep and covered himself and others with dirt: 'Cleanse me...and I shall be clean; wash me and I shall be whiter than snow... blot out all my iniquity. Create in me a pure heart, O God, and renew a steadfast spirit within me'.[3] Repentance, forgiveness and a restored relationship – all are possible for those who are tired of being splashed with the mud of the world outside or smeared by surprising uncleanness welling up from within.

Inner cleanliness comes first

Jesus warned that the bad thoughts of the heart are more contaminating than to eat with dirty hands or drink dirty water: 'The things that come out of the mouth come from the heart, and these make a man "unclean."'[4] David had learned this truth the hard way. The waywardness of his heart had led to a message that should never have been sent, followed by adultery that should never have happened. Then came a failed attempt to cover up Bathsheba's ensuing pregnancy by inviting her loyal and upright husband to come home from battle. The final order that caused Uriah's death might earlier have been inconceivable, but David was led away little by little by his uncurbed desires.

Although now a king, he was restored to his senses by Nathan's appeal to his shepherd's heart. He had acted like a rich man with a flock of his own to choose from, but who had slaughtered a poor man's pet lamb for a feast. This little lamb had grown up in the poor man's family and, to add to the poignancy of his tale, the prophet said that it had shared his food, drunk from his cup and even slept in his arms. At first blind to the parable, David burned with anger, until Nathan's 'You are the man!' hit its target.[5] Psalm 51 followed that. Many can empathise with David's shame and humiliation as he realised that what he had thought was a secret was now public property.

Now wash your feet

As well as being aware of such betrayers within, both Paul and James warned against being marked and marred by the murky values of the world outside.[6] Submission to the cleaning up operation is necessary each time such pollution happens. It is not good enough for a schoolboy to say, 'I had a shower this morning', when repeated falls onto a churned up football field have since covered him with mud. The dirt will spread unless he quickly does something about it. The boy can run off and clean himself up again, but we can't do that for our souls. Every day we are assaulted by mud slinging from our spiritual enemy.

Neglected sheep are prone to painful and putrid diseases of the feet and, unless treated promptly, will be crippled by them. The lambs of a flock are especially vulnerable and need special attention, a point to note again when applying the spiritual parallel. We are reminded of this by the episode at the Passover feast in the upper room.[7] At first Peter resisted Jesus' offer to wash his feet, this being too much for his pride to accept; but when his Lord explained that by rejecting this service he would break up their relationship, he then protested that foot washing alone was not enough – he needed a bath! Jesus assured him that this was not necessary as he had already been made clean by his response to his teaching.[8] Only Peter's dirty bare feet needed to be washed – the part of him contaminated by walking along the dusty earth, just as sheep are contaminated by what lies underfoot. As James said, we too risk being polluted by walking in the mire of the world.

Yet, as the Lord had forewarned Peter, it was only a few hours after he had sworn to be faithful to the death that fear came welling up from his heart and out came false words about the very relationship he had so much desired to cement. The opinion of very minor worldlings intimidated him and his former bravado was shown up for what it was. Convicted then by a straight look from Jesus as he was led away, Peter broke down and wept bitterly.[9] Later, repentant, he would meet with loving forgiveness and a fresh commission from the one he had denied. He was no longer to be a fisher of men but an under-shepherd.[10] The spoiled relationship was restored. He was clean again, and the same cleaning up operation can be ours.

We learn from our lapses, and out of his own bitter experience of defeat, Peter could later write to other forgiven sinners: 'You were like sheep going astray, but now you have returned to the Shepherd and Overseer of your souls'.[11] They had been lost but then responded to the sacrificial love of Jesus. They had been drawn into his fold, washed clean by him and were ready to follow wherever he led them. Peter himself was speaking as a soul restored, but the healing encounter on the shore was just the start of his transformation.

Restoring the image

The restoration of Peter to the discipleship Jesus had first called him to reminds us of God's intention when he designed human beings. We are told that he created us 'in his own image'[12] which conveys huge possibilities. However, as the Godhead is three persons in one, such imagery must include the capacity to form dynamic, interactive relationships, ideally with God as well as with each other. I suspect that the human newborn is unique amongst mammals in being able to look up into the face of a nursing mother from the start. (Think of suckling kittens, foals and others for whom this is a physical impossibility. Even a new baby chimpanzee's view is impeded during feeds by the mother's large jaw and flat chest.) Researchers into baby behaviour have shown for decades that, amongst other experimental patterns, the human newborn quickly shows a preference for the representation of a face, being especially attracted to eyes. Even more fascinating is that, when held in the crook of an arm, an infant child is at exactly the right distance to bring the parent's face into focus, and then follows the evident enjoyment of eye-to-eye contact.[13] Given enough of this, mutual attachment grows and the infant will quickly respond to the admirer with a smile. (The old wives' tale about windy smiles would be a myth at any age!) Pleasure in the company of others is thus a normal part of being human, right from the start. It is an important part of the reflection in us of the image of our triune God.

Sadly, I have also seen what happens when the relationship between child and parents never takes off, or is broken. In the early 1990s, when Eastern European tyrannies ended, aid workers had access to institutions previously unheard of where, amongst other horrors, they found myriad abandoned babies. With minimal physical care and without personal love, these children either failed to thrive or died. The lost look in their eyes was unforgettable, conveying a vivid picture of the despair of a soul out of relationship with the Creator. The same look can be seen on the faces of abused or abandoned older children, described by the great Dr Barnado as being 'like little lamps with the light gone out'. The light can only start to beam out again when love returns to their lives.

We were designed to live in a web of mutually loving relationships, the love of and for God himself being both source and supply. A clear idea of what this implies is found in our Lord, Jesus Christ, who was 'the image of the invisible God' personified, sometimes expressed as God made man.[14] Even when cleaned up a little, we will need a lot of restoration to approach *that* image. Yet if the headstrong, impetuous but cowardly Peter could be so much changed, there is hope.

The change in Peter and the other apostles began with the dramatic descent of the third person of the Trinity, the Holy Spirit.[15] They were no longer recognisable as their former selves and people were amazed. The Spirit of Jesus at work in and through them meant that they would never be the same again because they were being transformed to become more like their Lord – back into the image of God, as shown to the world in Jesus. The Warwickshire shepherds aimed to improve their flock by selective breeding, but this is a transformation that no merely human intervention can produce. There are no hybrids in this flock.

1   Luke 19:10
2   John 3:14-19
3   Psalm 51:7-10
4   Matthew 15:17-20
5   2 Samuel 11:2-12:7
6   Romans 12:2; James 1:27
7   John 13:3-10
8   John 15:3
9   Luke 22:54-62
10 John 21:15-17
11 1 Peter 2:25
12 Genesis 1:27
13 Kennell JH, Klaus MH. *Maternal-infant bonding.* St Louis: The CV Mosby Company, 1976.
14 Colossians 1:15
15 Acts 2:1-13

8

Restoration and transformation

Years ago I had under my care a young boy suffering from the great affliction of cystic fibrosis, a genetically inherited disease: wherever mucus is produced in the body, it is abnormally sticky and produces widespread problems, chief of which are recurrent chest infections and impaired digestion with poor weight gain. Current therapies prolong life, but sufferers tend to meet an earlier death than most of their peers.

Christopher was no exception. As high intelligence is commonly carried on the same gene, he deduced after being very ill that his disease was possibly life-threatening. Like many children, he did not speak up about his anxiety but it showed in his changed mood and episodes of asthma. Finally he said to his mother, 'This cystic fibrosis that I've got, can it kill you?' He was six and a half years old. What should she say? All credit to her, despite the shock of the question, she had the sense first to clarify what was being asked:

'Why do you ask me that, Chris?'
'Well, when I was ill in hospital you and Dad were worried
so I've thought about that, and now I'm worried, too.'
'What is it that worries you, Chris?'
'I'm worried that when I die I'll be cold and hungry in the grave.'
'Why, Chris! That will only be your body in the grave,
like an old overcoat that you've grown out of. *You* will
have gone to be with Grandpa.'

Immediately Christopher's anxiety subsided and his related symptoms ceased. A few years later, with greater perception, he replaced the analogy of the old overcoat with the idea of a chrysalis, one day to become a beautiful butterfly. Its caterpillar origin had been transformed. After good symptomatic control and some vigorous and adventurous years, a butterfly was eventually carved on the headstone of his grave.

All change

Students of the Greek New Testament tell us that the word translated 'transformation' has the same root as 'metamorphosis' and appears only three times. To think of the total change of chrysalis to butterfly or tadpole into frog is to visualise metamorphosis. The word is used to describe the transfiguration of Jesus witnessed by Peter, James and John. There was a dazzling change in his appearance, probably a pre-crucifixion sighting of his post-resurrection body.[1]

The next use of the word is by Paul, writing to the predominantly Gentile Christians in Rome. If the second part of Romans chapter one even touches on a description of the dissolute lives they had been saved from, they had a lot to learn and to unlearn. No wonder Paul urges them not to conform any more to the pattern of the world about them, but to be 'transformed by the renewing of your mind'.[2] The sickening norms of this first chapter of Romans must be sloughed off, just as the chrysalis splits and is shed by the emerging butterfly. Even then it takes a little time to soar up into the heights and flights it was designed for.

As when Paul was writing, so now. The minds of his readers must always be expanded by learning about the saving nature of faith in Christ, of the resultant peace with God and the gift of new life through his Spirit – for believing Gentiles and Jews alike. Then comes the prospect of polluted creation itself being released and made new along with redeemed humanity. All this and more Paul packs into the chapters leading up to his 'Therefore' of Romans chapter twelve, verse one. Therefore, take action. If you accept all that, then offer yourselves back to the loving God who offers to lead you out of the quagmire around you and to give you a new, clean mindset. 'Do not conform any longer to the pattern of this world, but be transformed by the renewing of your mind.'

Paul uses the same word, its third usage, when writing to citizens of another corrupt city, Corinth. He had just been reflecting on the times when Moses had to veil his shining face after meeting with God, lest he dazzle his people. Speaking again of the work of the Spirit, Paul then goes on to say, 'And we, who with unveiled faces all reflect the Lord's glory, are being transformed into his likeness with ever-increasing glory, which comes from the Lord, who is the Spirit'.[3] We are to undergo the metamorphosis of becoming like Jesus. Amazing! The transformation will be completed when Jesus returns and our resurrected bodies become like his.[4]

Transformed through the Spirit

Paul himself had undergone one of the most striking transformations recorded in the Bible. It is described in Acts chapter nine, where we first find him 'breathing out murderous threats against the Lord's disciples'. It seems that after witnessing the first Christian martyrdom, his blood lust was up. Freshly charged with murderous zeal and on his way to arrest and imprison other believers, he had his famous Damascus Road experience, and became a changed man. His personality remained recognisably zealous, but his diverted passion now was to spread the message of salvation abroad, not to try and stamp it out. Pharisee of the Pharisees, his commission and eventual mission was to the Gentiles, earning him the undying hatred of his earlier Jewish allies. What a complete *volte face*! He became the author of almost half of the New Testament, and much of it was written in prison. The theme of many of his letters explains how we, too, can be transformed, but rarely has this happened so dramatically.

Whilst we are still earthbound, the gradual change in our nature is only made possible through the gift of God's Spirit. We remember again that Jesus said, 'Whoever believes in me, as the Scripture has said, streams of living water will flow from within him', and John goes on to explain, 'By this he meant the Spirit, whom those who believed in him were later to receive. Up to that time the Spirit had not been given, since Jesus had not yet been glorified'.[5] After his ascension came Pentecost and the first indwelling of the Holy Spirit. The Spirit continues to revitalise those who have accepted Christ's atoning sacrifice and his gift of eternal life, defined by him as knowing both his Father and himself.[6] More than that, he 'flows from within' so that believers filled with the Spirit not only lead transformed lives themselves but also have an effect on the lives of others.

In another of his parables, Jesus likened the effect of the Spirit's work in someone's life to the fruit borne by a vine when sap flows freely through it.[7] Those who remain in unbroken communion with him, nourished by the Spirit, might well be unconscious of the fruitfulness of their lives, but it will be there. Instead of the outpouring of a defiled and egocentric heart will be found the wonderfully varied fruits produced by the Spirit, perhaps best summarised as love in action towards God and our neighbours.[8] This is in addition to the variety of gifts given by the Spirit 'for the common good', not all being given to all but distributed within the body of Christ 'just as he determines'.[9]

Changed lives speak louder than a lot of words, and will point others to the one who changed them.

Changed lives

Two people come to mind whose childhood experiences had turned them into adults with strikingly drawn and anxious faces. A few years after we first met, I saw each of them again. One had become a missionary in Africa and returned looking completely different. She told me that a 'chance' remark from a friend, although intended to tease her, had echoed a sharp rebuke she had repeatedly been given in her early days and which had left her feeling downgraded ever after. The same words coming from a good friend had acted as a key, unlocking all the pent up hurt of childhood. She had burst into tears, to her companion's understandable astonishment. That friend had unconsciously been prompted by the Holy Spirit to use a particularly emotive turn of phrase and the resultant catharsis had been like the discharge of an emotional abscess. The strikingly different relaxed and happy expression I'd noticed dated from that adult experience. The other woman had also been deeply damaged as a child, but since we first met had received counselling from a wise spiritual director and been helped to commit her life to God. She, too, emanated peace in place of her previous tension. Two lives had been transformed, the Holy Spirit acting in very different ways to release each of them from old hurts and empowering them in their wholehearted service for him. The release from her painful past had left each of the women with much greater sensitivity towards the hurts of others, and a loving concern to introduce them to the same healing Spirit of Jesus.

Some years ago, I saw an advertisement for a furniture restorer and went along to the shop with a broken chair which was a dangerous hazard and unfit for use. The restorer looked at it carefully, appraising the damage and the action needed. Then, a few weeks later I collected it. It looked like a different chair. The craftsman had restored it, not just to the well worn object it had been, but to a stronger, safer and more highly polished version. I noticed one more thing. He seemed reluctant to let it go, running his long, sensitive fingers over it almost lovingly, pleased with his handiwork and keen to check that no flaw had escaped his notice. Finally he handed it back, and I went off to recommend him to my friends.

Our Shepherd, once a carpenter in Nazareth, works on our

broken and damaged lives to achieve his ultimate goal, but he does not hand them back to us to try again on our own. For the rest of our lives we will feel the touch of his gently appraising and restoring hands as he continues to hold, strengthen and transform us into the people he wants us to be. By life and lip, whether consciously or not, we cannot then help but share with others the wonders of his works of love.

1   Mark 9:2-5
2   Romans 12:2
3   2 Corinthians 3:18
4   Philippians 3:20,21
5   John 7:38,39
6   John 17:3
7   John 15:1-8
8   Galatians 5:22-25
9   1 Corinthians 12:4-11,27-31

9

He leads…He guides in paths of righteousness

Eastern shepherds go ahead of their flock, leading them beside the still waters for refreshment and, after they feel stronger, preparing to guide them elsewhere. Nowadays, unless in very hilly country, western shepherds are almost as likely to be seen on quad bikes or tractors, steering their sometimes unwilling sheep wherever they want them to go, often assisted by a sheepdog or two. David was, of course, an Israeli shepherd but the principles of caring for sheep can be applied universally.

Gentle leading

'Leading' suggests a closer, less forceful involvement and is usually carried out slowly, on foot. As Handel's *Messiah* repeatedly reminds us (quoting Isaiah chapter 40, verse 11) 'he *gently* leads….' with particular reference to those that are with young. David speaks of being led beside quiet waters, suggestive of ambling along in a calm, unhurried manner. Gentle leading allows the sheep to stop and graze for a while before picking up the trail, and any that have started to stray are prompted to hurry back to stay within sound of the shepherd's voice.

It seems to me that this quiet, measured progress applies best to youngsters who, like me, have been given the great benefit of a Christian home and are able to remain under its influence until they have grown up a little. In their early days they are unlikely to be conscious of any more leading than that of parental or educational instruction and correction, yet these are quietly formative years when personality emerges, emotional attitudes are formed and the seeds of future interests are sown. I was also blessed in early childhood to be personally introduced to the Lord Jesus as my Shepherd.

Dangerous driving

In contrast, far too many children experience driving, not leading. They are dragged up, not brought up, to the accompaniment of loud voices and emotional storms. Worldwide, many are abducted and abused. There are no quiet waters for them. Gentleness is largely out of their experience so they are more likely to become rough than gentle, although some might be so cowed that, unless victimised by bullies, they attract little attention. Both wild and subdued children deserve to find teachers ready to understand their need for kindlier leading, but often fail to do so.

In Britain we are now seeing a generation of parents who, having had similar experiences in their youth, know little more about the conduct of family life than what they see on soap operas. They receive little wise counsel from their elders or support from their peers. After a violent quarrel that had also damaged their baby, I once asked a young couple if they had any friends. He said to her, 'You've got one, haven't you?' She replied, 'Who do you mean?'

Some Christian bodies, church based and otherwise, are providing friendship combined with better models through Mums and Toddlers groups, sports days for Dads and Lads and the like. Overseas, safe houses and children's homes can give added protection, treatment and training. All are hoping by these efforts to lay better foundations for the young lives they care for, but more under-shepherds are urgently needed, backed by prayer supporters. Even to be shown a little care can be a unique experience for some.

When the going gets tough

'Guiding' is more likely to be needed when the terrain gets rougher and the progress tougher. David was probably applying this kind of shepherding to himself, a grown man who needed help in choosing the right way to go. In his *Desert and Shepherd in Our Biblical Heritage* Nogah Hareuveni gives a wonderful description of the wilderness David knew and through which he would have guided his flock.[1] His accompanying photographs show a barren land, crisscrossed in a honeycomb pattern of countless interlocking grazing tracks. Each path provides a foothold for the animals through what is often dangerous terrain, where it would be very easy to come out on the edge of an abyss, or to turn the wrong way at a junction, go round in a circle, and so to get hopelessly lost. It is easy to see the connection with the crooked paths and devious ways contrasted in Scripture to 'the paths of the righteous'.[2] The shepherd does not stay aloof, ahead of such foolish wanderers, but gets alongside to direct them onto safer, straighter paths. David transposed this to his human straying and stumbling, saying, 'he guides me in the paths of righteousness for his name's sake'.

Keep to the right

A dictionary definition of righteous is 'to be just, upright, virtuous or law abiding in person, life or action' but it does not indicate the standard by which justice, for example, is to be measured. Our laws keep changing. In Britain, new restrictions regularly appear, whilst some activities counted as illegal a century ago are now viewed with more tolerance and a virtuous life often made a target for mockery. In some oppressive regimes it is an offence to practise any but the state religion, however virtuous or otherwise the practitioner's life might be. The enemy of souls is ever ready to pervert the right ways of the Lord. How can we determine God's standard of righteousness?

Sometimes, a steep and dangerous pathway has handrails provided to help the walker to climb up it without risk of falling. We recall that when asked by a lawyer to identify the most important commandment of all, Jesus quoted two great rules for life which would act as handrails to the righteous pathway. Firstly, 'Love the Lord your God with all your heart and with all your soul and with all your mind and with all your strength'. Secondly, 'Love your neighbour as yourself'.[3] His use of the word love was exemplified by his own lack of self-love and his total willingness to lay down his life for others. Such love will keep us in the paths of righteousness, but Christians all over the world know what it is constantly to need the Shepherd's guidance as they pick their way through the local quick sands whilst still trying to keep to godly paths. He acts as our compass, the one on whom we should fix our eyes, so that – inspired and enabled by him – we do not grow weary and lose heart.[4]

Like Peter at the Lord's last Passover meal, we need readily – and regularly – to submit our soiled feet to his careful attention. In addition, any of us could easily stumble across booby traps set by the enemy of souls that, when sprung, aim to cause the worst havoc of all to our varied relationships.

Have it your own way and see what happens

Having abandoned the twin commandments of love for God and neighbour, some societies are instead ruled by 'anything goes'. Whether personal, public or professional, before birth or approaching death, relationships form a most precious part of the image of our triune God in us. They are constantly under threat and vulnerable to damage and fracture. In supposedly developed societies, relationships between the sexes and with the unborn are the most threatened of all.

As I have been writing this, every one of the headlines of the morning's news detailed item after item showing this to be so. First came opposition to a new law in South Dakota, making abortion illegal unless the mother's life was at risk; those favouring abortion expressing their anger that 'the church' had influenced this legal decision. The next item was about a young woman and her then fiancé who, anticipating her infertility after surgery for cancer, had used in vitro fertilisation to procure frozen embryos. She wanted a child from this source, but their relationship had irretrievably broken down and the man involved refused to agree to the further development of a child to whom he would never act as father. Next came the report of the rape of an eleven year old girl by an unknown assailant, closely followed by a proposed parliamentary bill to convict a man of rape if the woman had been too drunk to give her consent. Later we heard how women were being sent from Britain to India for abortion of their baby girls which, having been identified by ultrasound, are considered less desirable than boys. Finally, a mother's heartbreak surfaced with a vicar's impressive honesty as she left her church ministry, unable to forgive the suicide bomber who had killed her daughter. She had not lost her faith but no longer felt it honest to preach peace and reconciliation to others whilst lacking a forgiving spirit herself. So the sad saga went on, story after story reminding us how, on so many fronts, conflicting interests assail human relationships.

Seek peace and pursue it

There were other news items, of course, about international conflicts, terrorism, ethnic cleansing, big business corruption, supermarket takeover bids and so on; these features simply underlined my point on a grander scale. I recall a newscaster who failed in his admirable attempt to put on a 'good news show' but he is no longer seen on our screens. Yet coincidentally (or perhaps providentially), wrapped around that bad news day were three television programmes in which Archbishop Desmond Tutu was shown on a 'truth and reconciliation' panel. Perpetrators of shocking crimes on either side of the armed struggle in Ireland met the individuals and bereaved families they had so badly hurt. There was much plain speaking and vented feeling but also deep communication and growth in mutual understanding, ending with a degree of reconciliation instead of total recrimination, even after a half hour exchange. The gentle persistence and encouragement of Desmond Tutu was like oil on the wounds and it was clear to this viewer at least that this was the work of God. Only he can enable us to foil the attacks of the enemy, and only he can guide our steps along the paths of righteousness.

This is not to say that our Shepherd will never take us into battle areas. As news bulletins remind us every day, wherever we are, we live in such war zones. Neither do we always know with absolute confidence which side is truly righteous. We surely do need to be guided aright and to find and establish principles on which to make sound judgments. We are no longer young children, judging by appearances, and have to learn to weigh up options, perhaps as we balance one apparent good with another. Thankfully, David already gives us a clue as to the source of such principles and the reason we need to live by them. Guidance in the paths of righteousness is for 'his name's sake', so we must not pursue a trail that would end by dishonouring his name.

God's offer of wisdom

Both Old and New Testaments speak of God as being utterly righteous. Thus, Jeremiah spoke in the context of good shepherding as he looked ahead to the reunion of the scattered Israeli flock under one wise and just leader, giving him the title 'The LORD Our Righteousness' – righteousness personified.[5] Paul expanded this for us: 'This righteousness from God comes through faith in Jesus Christ to all who believe'.[6] As the old hymn puts it, 'He died to make us good', when we put our faith in Jesus Christ. He has redeemed us, paid the price to bring us back to a personal, unclouded relationship with God. Further, Paul's first letter to the Corinthians tells us how believers 'are in Christ Jesus, who has become for us wisdom from God – that is, our righteousness, holiness [in other words, consecration] and redemption'. The passage ends with a warning against boastfulness on any other basis, especially of being reliant on human wisdom instead of giving a demonstration of the Spirit's power.[7]

Stringing together all Paul's pearls in this part of his first letter to Corinth, we find that the triune God, through faith in the Son, offers his humble followers (as part of his image in them) his own great wisdom. This enlightens their obvious inadequacies and shames those whose supposed wisdom is only the wisdom of the world. It is the power of God's Spirit that will have this effect, not our own persuasive arguments about rights and wrongs. Only he can clarify the issues that perplex us.

What would Jesus think and do?

Paul's awestruck conclusion to his Corinthian readers was that, through God's Spirit, 'we have the mind of Christ'.[8] We might therefore expect Christian thought to run counter to the received wisdom of a secular and rationalistic culture, and indeed this is so. In *New Issues Facing Christians Today*, John Stott details many of these differences in outlook, including issues global, social and personal.[9] Christian thinkers and writers should not expect to be *Top Of The [world's] Pops*, but can be confident that God accepts all who fear him and do what is right.[10] He is still able to do immeasurably more than we can ask or imagine, according to his power at work in us.[11] Our part is to be humble enough to be guided and to keep plugged in to that power, instead of trying to go it alone. Yet, as we are to love him with mind as well as all else, his mind will teach ours to grapple with some of the uncertainties we face. The ways in which the Good Shepherd guides are learned by experience and will have individual variations.

As we learn to know our Shepherd's voice, we can be sure that we are not hearing him if we set foot on paths of unrighteousness or even of self-righteousness. The paths of his righteousness might at first seem narrow and sometimes hazardous to the uninitiated, and other tracks more beguiling. Faithful following calls for committed wills and self-control, not the deliberate turning of deaf ears. Yet assurances of the Shepherd's constant care, and mounting evidence of his wise direction, gradually encourage us to practise his presence prayerfully and to develop greater sensitivity to his prompting. He might not hand out blueprints, and we will not travel as though on automatic pilot, but he has his own ways of nudging us along in the right direction. To sense these nudges at times of uncertainty we must learn to be alert to them.

Trust and obey

Many years ago, at a time when I was feeling very uncertain about which way to go, I attended a children's service. A number of youngsters were taken up onto one side of the dais in front of us and were all blindfolded by their teacher. After scattering various obstacles across the space between them, the leader took his place on the other side. He then called each child in turn to come to him, giving careful instructions to turn to the left or right in order to avoid the obstacles they could not see. They all reached his side safely and not one of them had stumbled – the outcome of their trust and obedience. We were reminded of the promise, 'When you turn to the right or to the left, your ears will hear a voice behind you, saying, "This is the way;

walk in it."'[12] I could not have been alone in finding comfort and reassurance that I, too, could depend on being safely guided by the divine voice as I waited, expecting God to lead me along the pathways of his choice.

> *To him who is able to keep you from falling and to present*
> *you before his glorious presence without fault and with great*
> *joy – to the only God our Saviour be glory, majesty, power and*
> *authority, through Jesus Christ our Lord, before all ages, now*
> *and for evermore. Amen.(Jude 24)*

1   Hareuveni N (translated by Frenkley H). *Desert and Shepherd in Our Biblical Heritage.* Jerusalem: Neot Kedumim, 1991.

2   Proverbs 2:15,20

3   Mark 12:28-31

4   Hebrews 12:2,3

5   Jeremiah 23:1-6

6   Romans 3:22

7   1 Corinthians 1:18-2:5

8   1 Corinthians 2:16

9   Stott J. *New Issues Facing Christians Today.* Grand Rapids, Michigan: Zondervan Publishing, 1999.

10   Acts 10:35

11   Ephesians 3:20

12   Isaiah 30:21

10

He leads...
He guides *me*

Books are written about the matter of personal guidance and the varied ideas of the different authors can confuse the earnest reader. Some say that God has a clear-cut plan for each life and we need to seek this out, otherwise we have failed his purposes. Others say that he leaves our careers to our own inclinations and common sense and that he is more interested in *how* we live than *where* we live. Yet in these days of short-term contracts, competitiveness in the workplace and huge unemployment, as well as an ever increasing divorce rate (amongst Christians too), the maze of possible paths can leave us very much in need of wisdom. We long for reassurance that we have a guide when important decisions have to be taken. Perhaps most of the time he *leads* as we quietly go about our daily lives but, for critical decision taking, he is more clearly alongside to *guide*. In my experience, clear guidance comes at important crossroads in life whilst at other times we are trusted to use prayerful commonsense, only to find later on that God had truly blessed that path as well when the outcome had been committed to him.

Hikers in some parts of Europe will be familiar with mountain routes clearly marked with signposts; but, instead of indicating the distance to be travelled, they give an estimate of the time to be allowed before arrival at the chosen destination. This is not the case with the routes offered to us by our Shepherd. He rarely offers a timetable for our journey. A wise old lady once told me that waiting on God is a life-long lesson and I have come to agree with her. It is not simply a matter of waiting for him to open a door, though that can be what he does, but it is the development of an attitude of complete trust in his overall care for our needs, with his knowledge of what is best for us, and his *forte* for perfect timing – that is, waiting on God himself and wanting his glory, not our own.

Most of us need a lot of lessons before being able to relax into his love without being tempted to worry. At a particularly fraught time of uncertainty one such lesson came to me over the radio as ethereal voices sang, 'Rest in the Lord, wait patiently for him', and my swivelling inner compass returned to its fixed point. In a late nineteenth century meditation based on this verse, Andrew Murray commented: 'Seek not only the help, the gift thou needest: seek *himself*; wait *for him*. Give God his glory by resting in him, by trusting him fully, by waiting patiently for him. This patience honours him greatly; it leaves him, as God on the throne, to do his work; it yields self wholly into his hands. It lets God *be God*…Whether it be in the shorter specific periods of waiting, or as the continuous habit of the soul, rest in the Lord, be still before the Lord, and wait patiently'.[1]

For those who experience times of darkness in their waiting, not attributable to their own wrong-doing, there is encouragement from a late twentieth century writer: 'By waiting in quietness and hope through these times, many have found themselves nearer to God and more aware of his presence. Indeed, these times of darkness or the apparent absence of God can be seen as normal parts of the process by which we are led closer to God'.[2]

God was thinking yesterday of your tomorrow

The pattern of God's leading is better seen through that great instrument, the retrospectoscope. Through it, as CS Lewis once said, we see how 'A secret Master of Ceremonies has been at work'.[3] Many callings bring repeated exercises in trusting him for the next move, be they personal or professional. Do we pray about which of the many doors to try? In such a competitive world, do we trust him to lead to a suitable post? The experience we glean, the colleagues we have and the contacts we make will all be woven into the pattern of our lives and can have important implications for the future. It need not be stressed how true this is when seeking a partner for life.

God alone sees the end from the beginning, and was thinking yesterday of our tomorrow. How important that we ask him to lead the way and then follow that lead. It is likely for each of us that there will be times of uncertainty and even of unemployment. Closed doors might be one way in which our paths are directed. These setbacks do not mean that we are off the path of his blessing, but they give us another opportunity to practise patience and trust. Yet he has a way of making dead ends open up and finding ways round apparently insuperable obstacles, even at the last minute. Each experience of his leading will encourage us to trust him more next time.

God's waiting rooms

The Bible contains many injunctions to wait on the Lord and gives plentiful illustrations of people who did so.[4] Abraham had to wait for the birth of Isaac, Jacob served time to marry Rachel, Joseph waited from his teens to his thirties to be released from prison, and Moses died at 120 years of age after a life neatly divided into three stretches of 40 years, in each of which he learned patiently to wait on God in a variety of circumstances.

In the first chapter of Luke's gospel we read of Elizabeth and Zechariah, who for years had prayed for a child, just as the nation of Israel had for centuries waited for the Messiah. Now their son John was to announce his arrival. In the next chapter Luke also tells us of Simeon. He had been given a specific promise from God that he would live to see that same Messiah, but he was very old before his expectation was fulfilled and he received a prompt from the Spirit to visit the Temple. There he took the infant Jesus in his arms and his long wait ended.

God is not in a hurry and does not waste experience

Perhaps especially in today's world of extraordinarily rapid communication, we frequently have the urge to get a move on but heaven's traffic lights often seem to be stuck at amber – 'Wait!' Yet we are not simply being told to sit there passively, waiting for something spectacular to happen. We just have one description of a burning bush, out of which came a clear voice delivering a programme for the rest of a life, and that only came after Moses had served time in the wilderness for the second of his forty-year stints. In turn, we are called to wait expectantly on God himself, open to him for whatever he wants to do with our lives, the proviso being that we might bring glory to him, in life or in death. It is then up to him what happens.

For some this might mean a lifetime (or what might feel like a lifetime) spent in one place in a seemingly humdrum job. This is perhaps how Moses felt in those middle years, but later his detailed knowledge of desert life would be so valuable to a whole nation. God never wastes our life experiences, even when, like Moses, we have brought them upon ourselves.

As I write, a young woman has just told me of being shocked to find that a promising relationship has failed, an exciting work opportunity has foundered, and she is left facing an apparent brick wall. Yet she added, 'I have learned something I only knew before in my head: God loves me'. There are lessons to be learned in God's waiting rooms that we would miss when engaged in hectic activity.

We are primarily human *beings* not human *doings*. He has designed us for a relationship with him as a priority and that should govern all that we are and gradually become.

Some are able to tell stories of waiting on God that has meant actively committing to him some imminent crisis, or an approaching deadline that finally demands a vital decision or intervention. In Acts chapter twelve, we read how the young church in Jerusalem was praying earnestly about Peter's imprisonment and threatened execution, but when he was miraculously released and knocked on their door they didn't believe it! They had not learned to expect the unexpected from God. Yet it is up to him to answer prayer and overrule as only he knows best.

Jesus himself gives us the best model we have for committing to God something that we would prefer to have more choice about. His agonised prayer in the Garden of Gethsemane was for the bitter cup coming his way to be taken away; 'yet not my will, but yours be done'.[5] The outworking of his Father's will meant our salvation, but the Son had to decide to go through with the agony of it, and did so. As a friend of mine once put it, when facing painful but life-saving treatment, 'The only thing to do with a bitter cup is to drink it down'.

Special verses

Meanwhile, we are called to active waiting not mere resignation. The habit of daily Bible reading and prayer should gradually sensitise us to the Holy Spirit's words of encouragement or direction, which he then underlines as being for us. In time, certain verses will become very special to us, whilst others might light up only once in a lifetime.

Years ago, before going for an interview for a GP partnership, my morning reading contained a warning against making a covenant 'with the inhabitants of the land whither thou goest, lest it be for a snare in the midst of thee'.[6] Despite the fact that I was only going from Hertfordshire to Warwickshire for the day and that the 'inhabitants' were good Christian doctors (and in any case the whole passage was about God's covenant with Israel so was really nothing to do with me), those words leapt out of the passage. It was not that I was twisting its meaning to suit my inclinations, for I was in a hurry to be off and probably not 100 percent attentive. In the end there were other reasons for declining the invitation to move to what would have been professional green pastures, but that earlier illumination confirmed in anticipation what the final outcome was to be. Instead, I ended up at the seaside in a job that set my future course in a totally different direction, but that is another story.

At other times, an apparently chance encounter, an unexpected invitation, or the bewildering closure of a planned route can be his way of steering us in a new direction. We can rely on him to be faithful, and the reason for his faithfulness is his love. For him to behave otherwise would be inconsistent and contrary to his good name. When he leads and we trustingly follow, this brings praise and glory to him. Finding a path he will bless is indeed 'for his name's sake'. Even when we go forward, prayerfully but still in some uncertainty, the imagery of the sheep tracks in the wilderness, with their intersections and cross-connections, reminds us that our Shepherd can easily call us back, either onto the original track or to another one that he will also bless and prosper.

Know yourself
As we gain experience, our Lord gives us more freedom to judge for ourselves, as long as this is not done in a self-willed way or merely for personal gain. Primarily, choices are to be made for his name's sake. We are not automatons, simply obeying orders, but have been given minds to use in decision making. In time, as we get to know ourselves better, we might realise that there are some things for which we are temperamentally unsuited, or that we are indecisive by nature and need a push before taking the plunge. Commitment anxiety may have become habitual, in which case a wise counsellor might help to track it to source. Greater clarity might come as we first list and then weigh up pros and cons.

We look for some assurance that we are making a wise choice, but sometimes a sense of peace comes after the step has been taken, not before. Prayerful discussion with a more experienced Christian friend can be helpful both before and after the die has been cast.

Moving in a different direction
It is rewarding to study the way Paul and his companions got to Macedonia.[7] This would turn out to be a key move in taking the good news to the edge of Europe, yet Paul's original plan had been to go about half that distance, delivering messages from the Jerusalem elders to places visited on his first missionary journey. That task done, he did not immediately go back to base, although he was obviously uncertain which direction to take next. He tried a number of doors, but either had a strong sense of being on the wrong track, or the Holy Spirit acted in some other way to close those doors and to change his route. He was in the company of praying friends – a helpful hint for us – and finally received a direct call.

Paul's call was in a vision, whereas ours might come in a phonecall or letter. For him, this was the signal he needed and they got ready at once to leave for Macedonia. In summary, he had been commissioned to do a job, completion of which left him free to take a different direction. Tuned in to the Holy Spirit, and no doubt praying with his friends, he received a clear call and, without further delay, obeyed.

To be or not to be?

As a young person I was privately offered what I thought at the time was a plum job in a new area of my chosen specialty but was troubled about my motives should I immediately accept it. I consulted an older, wiser Christian who pointed out that this was either a heaven sent opportunity or a temptation: all I had to do was sort out which it was! So it was back to prayer for wisdom. Almost at once I was surprised to see the post advertised, a better way of going about things, and I was happy that the decision would rest with the interviewing panel. In the end, the job was mine and proved to be a very tough assignment, but through it a new direction opened up which led step by step, via Uganda, to my ultimate position. In addition, the post provided invaluable experience and special friendships, including one that would forge strong links with Australia.

Yet what if I had not, after all, applied? That was not the only post in the world, and I feel sure that our heart allegiance matters to our Lord even more than exactly whereabouts we are working. If he should have a specific something in mind for us to do, he is quite capable of taking us to it along another pathway. The important thing is that we are ready to allow God to work in us to will and to act according to his good pleasure.[8]

What if I refuse to follow?

It is possible and, at certain crossroads in life, probable, that another route will look more attractive and we quite simply do not want to go the way that we had sensed the Shepherd was taking us. We can rationalise our choice as, 'This other way would use my skills better', or, 'Someone else would be much more suitable for this', when the basic reason is, 'I just don't want to go there'. We can pray for divine guidance when it is already being made plain, or for miraculous intervention to stop us in our tracks when we had already been confident of his direction thus far.

It is likely that if we do not face our desires and excuses with him honestly and prayerfully and go right ahead, there will be a deep down sense that we are on the wrong track, however attractive and rewarding it might still seem. Perhaps by then we would feel humiliated, or cause inconvenience to others if, by confession and repentance, we should want to go back. To realise that it would have been wiser to obey is a lesson for life and, the lesson learned, he will shape the consequences as he sees best in those particular circumstances. Whatever that might mean, we can rest on the promise that *(my emphasis)* 'in *all* things God works for the good of those who love him'[9] – even when they have had to be *re*called according to his purpose.

There are certain other Christians who think that it must always be godlier to choose the hardest route but if instead they learn to look for his signs, they can find themselves surprised by joy. In a piece entitled *Self-fulfilment*, Cardinal Basil Hume addressed young men wanting to learn obedience and said: 'Perhaps it helps if we distinguish between being resigned to the will of God and surrendering to his will. The word 'resigned' suggests putting up with something, bearing it. 'Surrendering' – even though the word has connotations of weakness – has much more the sense of acceptance, a voluntary acceptance, an embracing God's will, a going out to meet his will'.[10] A renewed mind will find this to be his good, pleasing and perfect will.[11]

Signposts on the path

Career choices are not for everyone, but at some time in life we are all likely to come to a point of decision. Whether this be about choosing a life partner, a house, a church, a mission or a country, whatever the nature of the crossroads, we should follow the advice of the old hymn and 'take it to the Lord in prayer'. Then, keeping alert, we might put out feelers or try a few doors, looking for his signals and sensitive to his nudges, including possibly significant prompts from his Word.

Thus, when the post in Uganda eventually came up, three letters arrived in one day suggesting that I apply. This shook me but I had recently learned that, although useful as a wake-up call, circumstances could mislead. I badly needed a prod to fully persuade me that such a major departure would be under the Shepherd's leading – and in the course of my daily reading, I felt urged to read *Daily Light*, not at that time my custom. There, in that day's selection, were all my guidance verses, one after the other! 'This is the way; walk in it' comes home with great force at such moments of illumination.[12] Subsequent events made me grateful for that clear instruction. Another year elapsed before confirmation of the appointment, and that only after strong crosswinds had arisen that almost blew me off course.

Sometimes the mists persist even after consulting prayerful friends and it can be wiser then, if this proves possible, not to make a major life-changing move until more light dawns. Unlike the estimates given for climbing up mountain trails, there is no foreseeable time for this to happen. The attitude in which we wait can itself speak to sceptical onlookers almost as much as the eventual revelation of what we were waiting for.

God's timing is perfect. Our part is to obey another of that special selection of verses: 'Commit your way to the Lord; trust in him and he will do this…Be still before the Lord and wait patiently for him'.[13]

1 Murray A. *Waiting on God.* Belfast: Ambassador Productions Ltd, 1997.
2 Ryrie A. *Silent Waiting* Norwich: The Canterbury Press, 1999.
3 Lewis CS. *The Four Loves.* London: Fount, 2002 (first published 1942).
4 Psalm 37:7; Isaiah 30:18
5 Luke 22:42
6 Exodus 34:12 (Authorised Version)
7 Acts 16:4-10
8 Philippians 2:13
9 Romans 8:28
10 Hume B. *Searching for God.* London: Hodder and Stoughton, 1979.
11 Romans 12:2
12 Isaiah 30:21
13 Psalm 37:5,7

Walking *together* through the valley of the shadow of death

I can rejoice in the Shepherd's clear leading and share enthusiastically with others that he never fails – until suddenly he seems to have led me into a blind alley.

Does the rejoicing then stop and trust evaporate? Whatever the initial impact might be and however I have arrived there, this is a time to discover that our omnipotent Lord does not lead into blind alleys, yet he sometimes allows us to enter dark valleys. At times it can seem that the long, dark uncharted way will last forever, and that I might even die there, if only I could. A fallen sheep, lying on its back (a shepherd would say 'couped') *will* die unless someone helps it up, but just as a vigilant shepherd comes to the rescue and puts it on its feet again, so it is with the Good Shepherd. He is with me. A human shepherd cannot be there all the time, but my Shepherd never leaves me.

In his shepherding days, David would have led his sheep through the desert, its white flinty stones dazzling in the sunlight. A wandering, half-blinded sheep might find its track suddenly ending on the edge of a black abyss, or when following a wadi find itself scrambling along a rocky, dried up riverbed between terrifying cliffs and crying out in fear. A sheep could also have entered a valley imperceptibly, wandering on without waiting for directions, or more precipitately by running after other (or another) wayward sheep. In such a treacherous landscape, any unguarded step could bring with it the risk of falling, or worse. Well might this be called the valley of the shadow of death.

Death is not the only valley

It seems though that David's shadowed valley does not refer to death itself, as the fifth verse speaks of enemies and none of those can touch us in the hereafter. Yet even to speak of the shadow of death conveys a picture of fearful loss, of grief and of gloom. The dark night of the soul might be precipitated through the loss of loved ones, whether by death, dementia or the painful experience of rejection after a deliberate withdrawal or disappearance. It can also attack as an illness, or in the slow loss of hopes (even of hope itself) as we are taken into an experience of desolation and deprivation hitherto unknown.

It is true that oppressive darkness does sometimes come to some who realise that their earthly lives are ending, a time when even a previously strong faith has been known to falter. This is when under-shepherds can bring encouragement with reminders of God's unfailing promises. One such shelter in many a storm of doubt is that firm assurance, 'Never will I leave you; never will I forsake you'.[1] In feebleness we might falter, but he has promised that his hand will never lose its hold on any he knows as his own.[2]

Do I react or respond?

Years ago, as we arrived at our destination in my car, I recall how Professor Donald Court lingered for a few minutes more as we finished our conversation. He was an eminent Quaker and paediatrician whose views on community childcare were not always well accepted, and it was in this context that he pointed out to me the difference between reaction and response. He used for illustration how few were those who had responded to Jesus' earthly ministry and how the reaction of the majority had been to crucify him. Given time, some of them began to think differently, but hasty reactions remain commoner than considered responses.

It is possible for a completely unforeseeable valley experience to have me taken aback, perhaps reacting with resentment and bitterness to compound my natural grief. Such a reaction would indicate that it is about time that my complacency, perhaps my self-righteousness, was brought up short. The sides of a dark valley are so steep and awesome that a lost and crying sheep must feel woefully small and intimidated there. I, too, can only cry out in the new and painful awareness of my own inadequacies, at last shown up in the face of such difficulty, darkness and danger. It can seem that life has fallen about my ears in pieces, with dreams shattered and sorrow, failure or emptiness all that lies ahead. I can no longer see the track, or if I can it looks far too lonely and forbidding to follow further. My answers are no longer slick, my confidence no longer in myself – and where has the Shepherd gone? Just as a crow goes for the eyes of an enfeebled sheep, it is then that the enemy of souls will try to blind me to that continuing presence, so leaving me fearful and even doubtful of his love.

Yet at such a time it is good to reflect that just as the shadow of a wolf is not a wolf (however fearsome) so the shadow of death is not death. I do not need to fear the shadows, however real they might seem, when our resurrected Lord has conquered the substance. The presence of a shadow across the path means that, however unbelievably, the sun is still shining elsewhere. Indeed, the shadow might have fallen precisely because I have had my back to the light. Even when the darkness seems total, my response can be to trust that the one who burst forth from the grave will finally break through this as well. However I reached this place, there is no possible evil, without or within, that our Good Shepherd is powerless to keep at bay or to slay. He is a match for them all.

I can either react to the difficulties in ways that only add to the pain, or I can respond to the nail-pierced hand that has allowed them. It can take time to make the change, for the spirit might be willing but my emotions have left me too weak for much more than SOS prayers. Some comfort comes from Paul's testimony of the solace found in his valley: 'But he said to me, "My grace is sufficient for you, for my power is made perfect in weakness."'[3] Even a heavy heart can respond to that.

One answer to 'Why?' is 'Wait'

At times like this, it is also some comfort to know that, in his own darkest valley, the crucified Lord cried, 'Why?'[4] I can see now the answer to his question in the light of his resurrection and my salvation; he sees already the answer to mine. Whatever the feelings, the fact is that as then, so now, he loves me with unfailing love. His presence will never fail. His power will open up the way and bring me out into the clear again. I cannot fly out of this valley on the wings of a dove, nor run away from it, but *I will walk through it*, step by step, with his help. Perhaps only then will I realise how, in this dark, strange, confined and fearful place, I have slowly come to know the Shepherd more personally than I have ever known him before. I can no longer be objective as I describe his role.

One Sunday morning I was invited to a Jewish synagogue to join a group who were discussing this particular psalm of David. It was there that I was introduced to the writing of Nogah Hareuveni, and I remain grateful for that. It was a privileged and interesting experience in other ways to be in the company of students whose primary focus was on the Old Testament, and I was invited to join in the discussion if I wished. There came a moment when I felt impelled to speak, as one of the company said, 'I have never understood why in the fourth verse the psalmist changes from using the third person singular to the second'. 'Why!' I found myself exclaiming, 'It's in life's valleys that we get to know him so much better. *He* leads and guides, but in the valley, *you* are with me'.

Yes, he is *my* Shepherd, and I have so far been happy to accept the many benefits he provides for all of us in his flock. Now he has proved himself faithful on a more intimate and personal level, when I have been in big trouble and utterly dependent on him. I'm getting to know him better because I've not just been one amongst many. We have walked this lonely way together. Whether I come out the other side to find myself face to face with my Lord and Shepherd, death behind and eternal life still stretching ahead, or whether the end of the valley finds me still walking beside him here on earth, the outcome is up to him. The certainty is that he is with me, all the way, and banishes fear. I will therefore fear no evil.

He knows the end from the beginning

The testimony of some who have also taken a valley road tells me something that I am not always ready to hear whilst still stumbling along in mine. Eventually I shall understand what the Shepherd has taught me through an experience that, whilst it was happening, I might simply have wanted to throw back in his face. Meanwhile, he knows where and why he is taking me through this gloomy place, and he will stay close. Yet one day, as some had tried to assure me would be so, I will finally come out into the clear to find that all that I had thought lost has either been given back, repaired and restored, or replaced by something even more honouring to him.

I often think of the imagery of the pearl. Starting as an uncomfortable piece of grit in the soft flesh of the oyster, it is slowly covered over with a substance that soothes the oyster's pain and eventually produces something of value to others. It seems to me that this special substance is comparable to the love of God, although it is often many 'days of my life' (perhaps even all of them) before I can see how he has overruled what seemed at the time to be total tragedy. Ahead lies a new awareness of his loving purposes, and a greater sensitivity towards others in pain. Until then, I cling to the assurance that he is still with me.

Holding on – and being held

Towards the end of my time in Uganda, an African nurse invited me to her home in a tall apartment building. She met me at the entrance, carrying her little boy, just a few months old, and as we got into the elevator she apologised that the light bulb had failed. It was a noisy ascent and conversation stopped as we went up in total darkness with many ominous clangs and clashes from the poorly maintained mechanism. No sound came from her baby but, as we reached their floor and the door opened, there he was, eyes wide with apprehension but now turning eagerly to the light with his arms still wrapped tightly round his mother's neck. She saw my glance and said with loving satisfaction, 'Ah, he fears the dark, so he holds on to me'. He was too little to know the psalm but he had just experienced, and illustrated, the message of its fourth verse!

> All which thy child's mistake
> Fancies as lost, I have stored for thee at home:
> 'Rise, clasp My hand, and come!'
> Halts by me that footfall:
> Is my gloom, after all,
> Shade of His hand, outstretched caressingly?
> 'Ah, fondest, blindest, weakest,
> I am He Whom thou seekest!'
> Thou dravest love from thee, who dravest Me.
>
> (The hound of heaven,
> Francis Thompson 1859-1907)

In time, I shall be able to look back and thank my Shepherd for all that he came to mean to me (and perhaps to others) because of the valley, but until then the moment by moment task is to reach for his presence and trust to his love.

I   Hebrews 13:5
2   John 10:28
3   2 Corinthians 12:9
4   Matthew 27:46

12

Your rod and your staff, they comfort me

The same Hebrew word can be translated rod, staff, crook, stave, club or even sceptre, all referring to some kind of stick and used variously and interchangeably. Whether or not David was referring to a composite rod-and-staff, or carried two sticks for different purposes, we cannot be sure.

Rods and staffs

David had killed a lion and a bear by striking them, which would indicate a fairly hefty implement. His stones and sling would be no use at close quarters, effective as they were against Goliath. He had his staff in his hand on that occasion, too, but one well-aimed stone was enough to bring the giant down.[1] Speaking through Isaiah, the Lord tells his people not to fear the Assyrians, who beat them with a rod and lifted up a club against them, suggestive of two sticks with different functions.[2]

Picture postcard portrayals of shepherds show them carrying the shepherd's crook, a long staff with a hooked handle, a replica of which is carried by a bishop as a token of his pastoral role. In agricultural practice, only shepherds among herdsmen carry a crook. Such a slender object would not catch or control a horse, cow or runaway pig, but to see a shepherd catch a sheep round the neck or leg and draw it back to his side is to see in action a perfect tool for the job. The staff or crook is not primarily designed to be a weapon but is used to draw in the sheep for some kind of closer care. A shepherd might also walk along beside a tired or nervous sheep, contact with his staff being a reassuring token of his faithful presence.

In a rather complex passage in Zechariah, the prophet took two staffs as he pastured the flock. Nogah Hareuveni, citing the original Hebrew, quotes this passage as, 'I got two staffs, one of which I named Pleasant and the other Destroyer, and I proceeded to tend the sheep'.[3] A small lamb can be hooked right up into the shepherd's arms with his crook – 'pleasant' indeed. Conversely, David's bear and lion discovered that his rod, or club, would rightly have been called Destroyer, a blunt and powerful instrument essential when the enemy was at close quarters. It could also be thrown into the path of a wayward sheep as a deterrent until it came within reach of the crook. As weapon or warning, the rod would have a sterner purpose than the staff.

Ezekiel speaks of sheep passing 'under the rod' as a check that all are present and correct. The shepherd's staff could then draw out a sick sheep, or one with an evidently rebellious nature, to be given special care and attention.[4]

Strong but sensitive

Whether David was referring to two items of equipment or one, he gives us two clear images, reminiscent of the passage in Isaiah where the Lord's powerful arm rules with authority, but is complemented by his tender embrace of the lambs.[5]

One of Rembrandt's last great paintings, *The Return of the Prodigal Son* now hangs in the museum of the Hermitage in St Petersburg. It spoke powerfully to Henri JM Nouwen of a wanderer (like a lost sheep) finding the way home and his book of the same title shares his meditations on the portrait.[6] On the cover, the portrayal of the father's two welcoming hands, one very masculine and the other very feminine, emphasises the same contrast of strength and sensitivity as can be found in David's rod and staff. Speaking of the Lord God, James commented that he is (*emphasis mine*) 'the one able to *save* and *destroy*'.[7] He has this dual role, represented by his staff and rod with their complementary functions.

In Psalm 23, David is speaking in the context of the valley, and how the rod and staff bring comfort there. Both are symbols of the Shepherd's care, even if some find it hard to sense his presence in the gloom. As the little Ugandan boy reminded us, his loving touch is a reality, even in total darkness. Yet David strangely suggests that this comfort is mediated through the Shepherd's two sticks!

The Word and the Spirit

Without being too fanciful, Phillip Keller likens the rod to the Word of God, both weapon and warning, and the staff to his Spirit, prompting and strengthening.[8] This is in line with the description of the 'sword of the Spirit' as part of the Christian's weaponry.[9] The double-edged sword of the word of God 'judges thoughts and attitudes of the heart', so warning of error.[10] As for the strengthening staff, Jesus promised before his death, resurrection and ascension to bring comfort to his disciples through the coming of the Spirit as a Counsellor (one who comes alongside to help, also known as the Comforter). The Spirit would be available to 'teach you all things and remind you of everything I have said to you'.[11] Writing to the Ephesians, Paul's prayer was for the Father to 'strengthen you with power through his Spirit in your inner being'.[12] Many who have stumbled through spiritual valleys will know how reassuring it was whilst still there to be reminded of his promises and so strengthened to hold on. At such times, Word and Spirit combine to bring comfort.

It is also in the valley that some, not previously familiar with the Shepherd's voice, start to cry out for him when facing some kind of crisis too hard to handle on their own. The cries can be angry as much as anxious, questioning his control or even his existence, although many might have arrived in the valley through their own – or another's – drunken driving, or a fatal lust for money, sex or power. The Shepherd can use such a crisis as a rod, selecting out those who might then be helped by an under-shepherd able to apply the Word of God, both as a warning and a welcome, perhaps quoting the words of Jesus: 'Go now, and leave your life of sin'.[13] 'Come to me…learn from me.'[14]

Coming through

Under-shepherds themselves might feel like crying out to him too, when watching with others whose hearts are breaking under a load of grief. Why has a loving heavenly Father permitted a car crash, a death in childbirth, the survival of a seriously disabled baby, or a wasting disease in a young person? Could he not have reached out and prevented these natural disasters? The rod and staff remind us that even though we cannot always understand his ways, authority blended with concern are two inseparable aspects of his character. If we care, he cares far more and (as the cross, resurrection and ascension so triumphantly show us) he can even bring great good out of great tragedy. Indeed, many of his under-shepherds received their training to come alongside as helpers because of their own valley experiences. They are then amongst the comforters willing to walk beside others in their valleys.

This was true for a vicar and his family whose testimony I heard as I was writing this passage. Rob was expounding Philippians chapter one where Paul speaks of his own attitude to suffering.[15] He had arrived in his new church to discover fairly soon that the congregation was not a prayerful one, so he and his wife made this a matter of prayer themselves. Soon afterwards, he developed leukaemia for which standard treatment proved ineffective. The only hope offered by his physicians was for him to undergo a bone marrow transplant, with all the pains of therapy and the possibility of failure that this choice would involve. Shared with his wife and two young children, the decision was taken that he would go for it and so began a switchback of hope, dashed hope and hope renewed. During this time, they all had to face the fact that he might not survive. Peace came through accepting that, whatever the outcome, they could trust God because their goal was for Christ to be exalted, whether by life or by death. 'For to me, to live is Christ and to die is gain' did not simply trip off the tongue but slowly became the true response of his heart.[16]

Meanwhile, the congregation learned how to pray! Others of us joined in prayer for God's will to be done, not merely our own. Three others had received transplants at the same time as his, and our friend was one of the two who survived. As we listened to him we realised that not only had he recovered physically, but also his ministry had been enormously enhanced by having come to know and trust the Shepherd so much more intimately in that long valley. Previously he had wielded the 'rod' of God's Word with great power and authority but, although by no means lacking in grace then, he now spoke with gentler encouragement and comfort, anointed by the Spirit of whom the staff speaks. Like his Lord before him, his words are now marked by an abundance of both grace and truth.[17]

It's too dark to see

There are other stories with a less happy outcome. In that same week that I had heard Rob's story, a young woman told me how she had lost her faith because her mother had died of cancer when they had all prayed, sincerely believing that God would heal her. The distinction between healing and curing is not always adequately explained. God is omnipotent, and of course is capable of intervention to remove the disease or prolong life but, as with Jesus' healing miracles, his deep concern is for the whole person. Death will come to us all, but he is able to heal the bitterness, or the fear of dying, or the other evils that might assail a dying person, whilst not always restoring to physical health even after the most fervent prayers. We cannot dictate to him what he is to do. 'No' is still an answer, and so is 'wait'.

Like our Lord's 'Why?' on the cross, the answer might come much later. Yet he is still there in the valley, ready to indicate his presence and speak words of encouragement as long as ears are not blocked by contrary voices demanding his more dramatic intervention. What could be more encouraging than to hear him say: 'I will not in any way fail you nor give you up nor leave you without support. [I will] not, [I will] not, [I will] not in any degree leave you helpless nor forsake nor let [you] down (relax My hold on you). [Assuredly not!]'[18]

Light dawns

As a paediatrician, I was able to observe how often parents who had asked the 'Why?' question when tragedy struck have, in time, discovered an unexpected answer. Years after having had to tell a couple that their baby's life would be very short, and briefly walking with them in that very dark place, the child's mother spotted me at a public meeting. She came over to make herself known, wanting to tell me that she and her husband had not been part of the fold at the time of the baby's birth, but had met the Shepherd in their valley. As a result, they had introduced 15 other members of their family to him, and she herself now led an annual meeting of 100 women, all wanting to know more about what it was that had changed their friend's outlook from grief to gratitude. They had come *through* the valley shadowed by death, with good news to share.

Rod and staff, Word and Spirit, authority and encouragement, truth and grace – all used by the God of all comfort, 'who comforts us in all our troubles, so that we can comfort those in any trouble with the comfort we ourselves have received from God'.[19] To give, as well as to receive comfort, is first to have known the need for it.

Spur and solace

Along a wall in my primary school was a copy of a section from the Bayeux tapestry, depicting the events leading up to the Battle of Hastings in 1066. As battle commenced, we could see representations of prancing, multicoloured horses, armoured men with lances, and a rider near the back evidently spurring on the rest. At the time we were told that this was King Harold, 'comforting' his troops with a prod from behind. As small children, we puzzled over that strange use of the word comfort, only realising in later life that it had once held a different meaning from the one we knew, being more suggestive of a prod than a panacea.

I have recently searched through a book, *The Bayeux tapestry*, in which page after page illustrates this wonderful Anglo-Saxon strip cartoon.[20] It was 230 feet long and wonderfully embroidered in a few simple colours, with a running commentary in Latin. Yet neither Stenton's book nor a complete reproduction of the tapestry from

Bayeux itself shows the oft-quoted portrayal of Harold, the comforter. Instead there is a picture of his one time friend but recent enemy, Duke William. It depicts him helmeted, armour plated and on a red horse, his Norman army already galloping off ahead of him, except for the last in line who has turned his head to look at William. The Duke is brandishing what looks like a truncheon, but which the text says is his mace and the dictionary says was either his staff of office or a spiked club. This section is entitled 'Duke William exhorts his troops to fight heroically'. It is fairly soon followed by another scene in which his half-brother Odon, Bishop of Bayeux, from the back of a blue horse, is wielding a longer and slightly curlier stick. Presumably this could be his pastoral crook, held at the ready to draw in, or perhaps berate, any soldiers slow to engage in the fight. He, too, is said to be encouraging them.

These combined methods of encouragement, with their equivalents of rod and staff, were to be overwhelmingly successful. Poor Harold was shot in the eye and killed, his troops routed. The victors in that fierce and fearsome conflict had been spurred on both by the one wielding his mace-cum-club, afterwards to go down in history as William the Conqueror, and by Odon the staff-bearer, whose name and title are less familiar but who is said to have inspired and supervised the creation of this remarkable record.

With increasing life experience, many of us learn that strength to keep going in the face of difficulty or danger comes from someone who is ready to join the fray with us, to support, inspire and urge us on. A challenge from a staff of office might not be as comforting as the embrace of a shepherd's arms, yet our Lord and Shepherd, with his rod and staff, acts both as spur and solace, encouraging as well as comforting us in our valleys. That is how we come through them.

I   1 Samuel 17:48-50
2   Isaiah 10:24
3   Zechariah 11:7 (original Hebrew translation)
4   Ezekiel 20:37,38
5   Isaiah 40:10,11
6   Nouwen HJM. *The Return of the Prodigal Son*. London: Dartman, Longman and Todd, 1994.
7   James 4:12
8   Keller P. *Shepherd looks at Psalm 23*. Basingstoke: Pickering and Inglis Paperbacks, 1976.
9   Ephesians 6:17
10 Hebrews 4:12
11 John 14:16,26
12 Ephesians 3:16
13 John 8:11
14 Matthew 11:28,29
15 Philippians 1:12-26
16 Philippians 1:21
17 John 1:14
18 Hebrews 13:5 (Amplified Bible)
19 2 Corinthians 1:3,4
20 Stenton F *et al. The Bayeux tapestry.* London: Phaidon Press, 1973.

13

You prepare a table before me in the presence of my enemies

Some commentators think that David suddenly changed his imagery in mid-psalm and switched to thoughts of a banqueting table spread for him, perhaps to celebrate a victory during his kingship, whilst hungry enemy captives stood by and watched him enjoying a sumptuous meal. Yet he was a shepherd before he was a king, and aspects of his shepherding still fit the picture that he portrays in the psalm. With Phillip Keller, I prefer to pursue this analogy.

Setting the table
An old friend of mine lived in a house in the countryside, surrounded by lush grassy fields. Every winter the fields filled up with sheep, brought down from the Welsh mountains, where heavy snow would have made adequate grazing difficult. In some countries, the opposite happens, and the sheep are led away from the sun-dried valleys of summertime to the higher tablelands, where meadow flowers bloom amongst the richly fertile grassland and later provide clean hay. After haymaking, even in the lowlands, the growing remnants of grass will be parasite free, making safe and tender food for newly weaned lambs.

Whatever the setting, boggy land must be avoided and a source of clean water provided. Potentially poisonous seedlings such as ragwort must be cleared and bracken cut back lest it blinds the sheep that eats it. Pregnant ewes need an enriched diet, so in temperate climes root vegetables are scattered about the fields with supplementary minerals provided for the lambs as well. So the shepherd has to think ahead as he prepares the 'table' suited to the different needs and ages of his flock. In the Parable of the Sower, Jesus used different imagery but still stressed the importance of prepared ground for the best results.[1]

As he prepares the pastureland, a good shepherd must attend to the third essential cited by the Warwickshire farmers (discussed in chapter six), namely the protection of his flock against predators. In Britain, these enemies are foxes, adders or scavenging birds. Elsewhere wild dogs, big cats or even one of David's lions can present serious threats. At intervals the shepherd needs to dose or dip his flock to keep them free of less easily seen parasitic infestations. His work is never ending. Mostly unaware of all this vigilance, the tired and hungry sheep emerge from the hard experience of the valley, ready to settle down to a good feed on the prepared land.

What's on the menu?

We are reminded by the human shepherd's care for all ages that spiritual care and good nutrition for the sheep of God's pasture should similarly be presented appropriately. Parents with young children, or those new to faith, might have to search hard to find somewhere that offers adequate and suitable nourishment. 'Newborn babes' need the simplest and most easily digested spiritual food in order to grow.[2] My own experience of Sunday school affected my spiritual growth for decades, if only by teaching me Psalm 23. Learning by rote might be frowned on today, but early learning lasts the longest. The more mature should be taking in solid food, such as that provided by Bible reading with supplementary notes, study courses, or perhaps by the preparation involved in teaching others – an excellent way to learn.[3]

Whatever the age, the basic source of nourishment is the same, the Word of God inspired and absorbed through the activity of the Spirit of God, with ever deeper lessons to be learned as life goes on.

Care for the carers and food for the waiters

It can give insight into restaurant management to ask those who bring food to the table whether they are provided with a meal during a long day of looking after others. The answer often explains their lean and hungry look. A good pastor will be aware of the importance of all-age teaching, but will also need personal nourishment and support.

When saying farewell to the Ephesian church fathers Paul suggested to them that the young sheep he was leaving needed their oversight as under-shepherds, but also warned that they would need to keep a watch over themselves as well as their charges, otherwise 'savage wolves will come in among you and will not spare the flock'.[4] Peter, ex-fisherman turned shepherd, also warned church leaders against common forms of such attacks, urging them to be '...not greedy for money, but eager to serve; not lording it over those entrusted to you, but being examples to the flock'.[5]

For this, pastors, too, need to feed on and respond to God's Word, taking time out to do so either at home or with others like-minded. This might mean deciding to say 'No' more often. Although a consequence of attempting to meet overwhelming needs, being busy can also become a status symbol. The fellowship of a team ministry or supportive prayer group would guard against the implicit hazards of a one man band. Leaders, too, need time in green pastures and spaces in the diary to allow it. Members of their flock should stay alert to this need, perhaps at times offering practical help to facilitate it. Discouraged pastors as well as denuded pastures need to be refreshed and replenished, otherwise the sheep will either fail to thrive or move on to look for food elsewhere.

Enemies, without and within

Readers of missionary magazines will know that many hard-pressed pastors in the developing world have neither the luxury of solid biblical training behind them nor the fellowship of anyone else like-minded to refresh them. For them, a letter or a personal visit can act as a tonic. They need both our prayers and our gifts, perhaps sent as reading or teaching material, for without checks and balances errors can so easily slither in like a serpent.

In certain regimes, local opponents can be ready to pounce, whilst others act as undercover agents, bent on defamation and destruction of pastor and flock alike. In his other psalms David cites as poisons for the human spirit the snake-like venom found in the lies of wayward, wicked and violent men and asks to be rescued from them.[6] Many of our persecuted brothers and sisters know all about this, although their endurance has often been used to stimulate church growth. Those of us with relatively easier lives can feel greatly humbled to think of their readiness to experience suffering for the sake of their Lord.

Yet it is the enemy within that often does most damage to leaders and followers alike, perhaps by the lures of money, sex or power, but also by an unwise or badly expressed remark. Both Paul and James agree that the mouth is a channel for poison itself, rather than, as for sheep, the route for its ingestion. James especially warns believers about polluted talk being like water flowing from a contaminated spring.[7] By implication, we should make sure that by studying and feeding on God's Word we find an antidote to the poisonous talk and attitudes so often swirling round us, and against which we are so clearly warned. Malice, deceit, hypocrisy, envy and slander all involve the tongue, and God's word says that we are to be rid of them.[8] The snide remark, the juicy piece of gossip, the half-truth or outright untruth about someone else, all must go. Those with a destructively critical spirit should remember that pointing the finger leaves three fingers pointing back at the critic.

Protecting the young

Like some of the hidden infestations harboured in long, soiled grass, it is the lambs of the flock who are most at risk for picking up polluted talk, although familiarity can too readily desensitise the most dyed in the wool churchgoer. Despite its breaking the third commandment, how often have we heard the expression 'My God!' from believing lips?[9] The gentle question 'Was that a prayer or a swear?' has been known to break that habit! All of us need humbly to follow Peter's advice to believers under pressure, 'that by doing good you should silence the ignorant talk of foolish men'. This, he says, is God's will.[10] Just as bad company corrupts good character[11] so keeping good company must help to improve it, and how vital this is for young people everywhere.

In an old book by Dr Allan Fraser, *Sheep husbandry*, I was intrigued to find a passage about Merino sheep.[12] Although now bred and crossbred in many other countries, they originated in the mountains of Spain and are noted for their fine wool. Their natural tendency is to roam as a large flock from one fine grassy area to another but, says Dr Fraser, 'they form a sort of camp at night, on the highest part of their ground, and may be certainly found there at daybreak next morning, lying so closely that they touch one another, the strongest sheep outside and the weak in the centre'.

All over the world, it is the young and weak, whether animal or human, who are most at risk of damage, danger and even death. They need special protection by their elders, who must not be too cosy in their own lofty huddle for this to be forthcoming. We have a lot to learn from Spanish Merinos!

All-Prayer

As life goes on we become aware of our weakest points and realise that the enemy of souls delights to go for them, time after time. We should check that we have put on the whole armour of God as described by Paul in Ephesians chapter six, protecting our most vulnerable areas from head (ungodly thoughts) to toe (ungodly paths). His final injunction is for us to 'keep on praying'. In John Bunyan's most famous book of the 17th century, *The Pilgrim's Progress*, the chief character Christian was assailed by all kinds of horrors before remembering that he had been given the powerful weapon of 'All-Prayer' to help him overcome them. Although the opposition did not immediately cease, he was finally enabled to overcome the demonic onslaught.

Prayer does change things. In 1993, government sponsored persecution was rife against Christians in a country where they were very much a minority, and many were so fearful that they denied Christ. Christians worldwide were called to pray, and since then it is reported that things have changed. Few deny Christ anymore, and though still persecuted this is notably less intense. Those in prison are leading unbelieving fellow prisoners to Christ, and the Gospel is spreading. Believers bless and pray for those who persecute them, and leave their judgment to God.

Prayer with others can be strengthening when feeling so enfeebled by the fight that we run out of words, but in his solitary state Christian managed to quote the verse of a psalm as a cry for help, and found fresh strength to go on. When in the wilderness Jesus was strongly tempted by Satan at the start of his ministry he, too, quoted Bible verses to defeat him, and so can we. The sword of the Spirit, which is the Word of God, together with All-Prayer makes a quick and powerful combination of defensive weaponry against the wiles of the enemy.

The Lord's table

There is another application of David's 'table'. Every week in the ritual of the tabernacle, twelve loaves of consecrated bread ('the bread of the Presence') were to be set out before the Lord on a table of pure gold before being eaten by the priests in the holy place.[13] Once when David was fleeing from Saul and desperately hungry, Ahimelech, priest of Nob had given him this special bread to eat. Unfortunately Saul's head shepherd had happened to witness this contravention and reported it to Saul, with disastrous consequences for the priest.[14] Perhaps this episode had come again to David's mind when writing about a table, prepared and shared in the presence of his enemies. He could not foresee that the Tabernacle, and the Temple that succeeded it, would become obsolete. In the far future, another table would be spread, where believers would eat and drink and be thankful for the greatest victory of all time.

In his earthly life Jesus knew well the Temple in Jerusalem but once he had offered himself as the perfect sacrifice for all time, the rituals of the Old Covenant were no longer needed. As our perfect high priest he fulfilled all that they had foreshadowed, and brought in a new covenant between God and man.[15] He adapted the old Passover feast, no longer to be kept in memory of God's miraculous rescue of Israel from Egyptian bondage, but instead a reminder to believers of their salvation from the slavery of sin. Our enemies have been defeated. We now approach the Lord's table, free to break and eat bread in remembrance of his broken body and to drink the poured out wine as a symbol of his shed blood.[16] We remember, too, that as resurrection and ascension to the Father's right hand followed this sacrifice, he is always there to intercede on our behalf.[17]

The old has gone, the new has come

In his little book *Passover,* Gordon Jessup points out the prophetic nature of the Passover ritual, and how Jesus adapted it.[18] An especially telling point is that at the end of the meal, the celebrant gives what is known as 'the sop' to the one at the table he loves the most. We recall how graciously Jesus gave it to Judas, despite knowing his treacherous plans for delivering him into enemy hands.[19] Today we continue to share this feast in grateful remembrance of the same love and grace extended to us through his atoning sacrifice. At the same time we celebrate (and dedicate) the new life that is now ours through the Spirit, who raised him from the dead.

To quote from William Temple's notable commentary, *Readings in St John's Gospel,* we are reminded that Jesus' body represented his full humanity whilst his blood was the life poured out, that it might be offered to God.[20] In our communion services we use the material elements of bread and wine to represent the reality of his broken body and shed blood but, being unchanged, they remain symbolic elements only – but such powerful symbols! Archbishop Temple comments: 'To 'eat the flesh' and to 'drink the blood' of the Son of Man are not the same. The former is to receive the power of self-giving and self-sacrifice to the uttermost. The latter is to receive, in and through that self-giving and self-sacrifice, the life that is triumphant over death and united to God. Both elements are needed for the full act of 'communion'. The life that gives itself even to death; the life that rises from death into union with God: these are the divine gifts....' To reject these gifts is to die, but to accept them is to live forever.

John Stott expresses more of these truths in his book, *The Cross of Christ.*[21] At the Lord's Supper, or Eucharist, we *remember* his sacrifice, we *partake* of its benefits (hence communion), *we proclaim* his sacrifice, we *attribute our unity* to it, and we *give thanks*: 'and in token of our thanksgiving offer ourselves, our souls and bodies as 'living sacrifices' to his service'.[22]

Think about these things

Those who love him are regularly called to this table. He has prepared it for us. We need to think deeply about all that this means, lest the feast should become a mere formality. His enemies and ours were vanquished at Calvary, though they have not yet totally vanished and remain ready for rearguard action, even as we come to his table. There we should confess how we have not always claimed his victory but instead offered the devil a foothold.[23] Repentance is met by his loving forgiveness, communion with him is restored, and fellowship with each other deepened, all at the same time. No wonder he said that we were to do this in remembrance of him and then, restored and strengthened, go on to serve him with lives energised by responsive love. As we offer them back to the one who has saved us at such great cost, we also accept that following him can include walking through valleys, as he did.

Though we are many, we are one body

I recall an Easter morning communion service in western Uganda. Drums had summoned us to an already packed church where a friend and I were squeezed into the choir stalls. As we knelt there, waiting our turn to go up to the Lord's table set before us, all we could see were feet walking purposefully forwards. Some were white and some black, some shod and others bare. There were old feet, young feet and children's feet. Clean or dusty, smooth or gnarled, slim or swollen feet, they were all heading for the table prepared before them. The feet told stories of experience and inexperience, hardship and sacrifice, health and infirmity, but overwhelmingly of glorious unity in diversity. When our turn came, we found that, as the presiding bishop offered us the bread and wine, he was addressing us each individually in our own language. Before our eyes and ears, the Good Shepherd's expressed hope was being partially fulfilled: 'I have other sheep that are not of this sheep pen. I must bring them also. They too will listen to my voice, and there shall be one flock and one shepherd'.[24]

At such times, the Lord's table becomes a special place of shared celebration and joyful thankfulness.

1   Mark 4:1-20
2   1 Peter 2:2
3   Hebrews 5:14
4   Acts 20:28-31
5   1 Peter 5:2,3
6   Psalm 58:4, 140:3
7   Romans 3:13; James 3:7-12
8   1 Peter 2:1
9   Exodus 20:7
10 1 Peter 2:15
11 1 Corinthians 15:33
12 Fraser A. *Sheep husbandry*. London: Lockwood & Son, 1949.
13 Leviticus 24:5-9
14 1 Samuel 21:1-7, 22:9-19
15 Hebrews 8:1-13
16 Mark 14:12-26
17 Romans 8:34
18 Jessup G. *Passover*. London: Olive Press, 1980.
19 John 13:18-30
20 Temple W. *Readings in St John's Gospel*. London and Basingstoke: The Macmillan Press, 1940.
21 Stott J. *The Cross of Christ*. Leicester: Inter-Varsity Press, 1986.
22 Romans 12:1
23 Ephesians 4:27
24 John 10:16

14

You anoint my
head with oil

Oil features in Scripture as being multipurpose: for the consecration
of people and things, for cooking, for fuel, for use as therapy or, as
with the oil of gladness, to signify joy. It is hard to see how most of
these uses relate to sheep!

With most of his personal valleys still to come, David was taken
from tending his flock to be anointed with oil as king-in-waiting.[1]
As we pursue his shepherding theme, his psalm suggests that the
tired sheep, now grazing peacefully after their hard journey, had
developed a new, unspecified problem for which the remedy was oil
on their heads. Perhaps we get part of his meaning as we read our
Lord's reproachful words to Simon the Pharisee, 'You did not give
me any water for my feet...You did not put oil on my head'.[2] Clearly
this referred to the refreshment needed after a hot journey on foot,
customarily offered by a thoughtful host. After the gloom and chill
of the valley, coming out into open pastureland and bright sunshine
might find sheep similarly hot and bothered, but it seems likely that
David would then lead them to shade or water rather than going
round with an oilcan.

Counter-irritation
It is probable, though, that a shepherd would apply medicinal oil
to sheep with specific disorders. The presence of a flock in a warm
and sunny spot would be sure to attract flies, as anyone will know
who has tried to picnic in such a seemingly idyllic spot. The so called
'Australian salute' abounds in a country full of animal stock, and
consists of waving a hand across the face in an attempt to swipe off
the prevailing cloud of flies, only partially deterred by the drover's
broad-brimmed hat and its dangling corks. Sheep, though, can do
little more than scratch or shake their heads as they try to disperse any

of the many kinds of fly bothering them. They pester the sheep and worse still lay eggs in the nose or under the skin so that the animals nearly go mad with irritation from emerging maggots. Untended, some will die. Their own counter-irritant of rubbing their heads and backs against a bush or tree risks more sores and scratches, and more flies. Today various kinds of insecticide baths and oil-based liniments are readily to hand, but David would only have had olive oil to soothe the irritation and the open sores. Made smelly with sulphur, it could also put off the flies.

Apart from those with the sweetest dispositions, most of us know what it is to be irritated, even if only when shut in a room with a mosquito. More commonly, the intrusive telephone, the interruptions when trying to concentrate, delays when in a hurry, or unpalatable background music – all of us have our own pet aversions that, even metaphorically, get our heads tossing, feet stamping or hackles rising and generally leave us feeling scratchy. Especially when under pressure, small things can sometimes – all too often – act as huge irritants and we are tempted to swipe out, upsetting emotions all round, including our own. Whose telephone manner has not changed dramatically when a dear friend's voice came on the line? Which of us has never needed to bite back an irritable or barbed comment? James rightly says that the tongue can start a conflagration.[3] Those who enjoy quick repartee need (life-long) practice in controlling the mind before opening the mouth.

We tend to blame external agents for our irritability, but Jesus pointed to the heart as the source of our damaging words.[4] For sheep the shepherd's oil is for external application only, but the Spirit of the Good Shepherd anoints hearts and minds to calm our natural irritability with the gentle lubricant of his peace.[5] The Holy Spirit is given when a life is first committed to God by trusting in and responding to the saving work of the Lord Jesus Christ. The Spirit is poured into obedient lives as a guarantee of what lies ahead.[6] His desire is to fill us and overflow from us, but as someone has said, we leak! We need regularly to come back in repentance, especially when hit by sudden irritation, asking for his fruits of patience and self-control to replace our lack of both.[7]

Putting our heads together

Sheep are not noted for great thoughts, but they are vulnerable to a highly contagious skin disease, spread as they rub their heads together. They quickly lose wool and become sick and dishevelled, urgently needing whole body immersion in insecticide. We, too, can pick up practices, language and ideas by too much interaction with those who do not follow the Shepherd's wise leading so that our spiritual lives get out of condition. It is better to have our closest friendships and enjoy fellowship with those of his flock who regularly go to him for cleansing and anointing by his Spirit. The exchange of ideas is then under his guidance and not merely a reflection of the wisdom of men.[8]

Under the Spirit's influence, emotions, mind and will are all to be transformed – metamorphosed – into the likeness of our Shepherd himself. We should note that he included the *mind* as needing to be involved in expressing our love for God.[9] Mediated through his Spirit, divine wisdom is available to guide us about how best we can also show neighbour love. Such discernment is one of his many gifts.

Courting trouble

In an increasingly secular society, godliness is being lost and the wisdom of men relied on for law making, decision taking and the making and breaking of contracts, whether professional or personal. In Britain, laws were once based on the Ten Commandments and the Golden Rule of loving one's neighbour as oneself, but this is subtly and stealthily being changed. This often (if not usually) happens through the opinions of those exercising worldly wisdom and who, like young children, judge mostly by appearances.

We can each apply this to the particular field of affairs best known to us, but as I consider the world of medicine the number of dilemmas constantly increases, with difficult decisions to be made about matters of life and death, the appropriate allocation of resources, or both. Today, when there is serious disagreement, more cases are being taken to court for settlement by a judge. He or she will certainly be a qualified lawyer but is not always well versed in the intricacies of the debate; even expert witnesses can get it wrong. Jesus rebuked those who judged by mere externals and arrived at the wrong conclusions[10] but we now see this happening more and more for those whose appearance is judged to be against them.

By abandoning the divine wisdom that created us in his image (the image of a triune God whose selfless interrelationship is an important part of that imagery), and by being disobedient to his two great laws of love for God and neighbour, our advisers are becoming like 'infants, tossed back and forth by the waves, and blown here and there by every wind of teaching and by the cunning and craftiness of men in their deceitful scheming'.[11] Strong words! It will need those mature in faith and principle to stem the tide. This will only happen as we ask for the Holy Spirit to anoint the heads and give strength to the voices of those on the front line as they seek to put into practice the principles already given. Paul ends this passage with a call to build up the body of Christ in love, 'as each part does its work'.[12]

Worldly wise can be most unwise

Sensitive ten-year olds can exercise empathy and altruism, especially if they have needed such understanding themselves, but trained adult minds sometimes seem to have relapsed into more juvenile thought patterns. Glanville Williams was the author of a famous textbook on criminal law and his obituary acclaimed him as a brilliant and distinguished academic. He evidently believed that he was showing empathy with a Down's baby whose early death had been expedited by his paediatrician when he wrote: 'If a wicked fairy told me that she was about to transform me into a Down's baby (or Down's adult) and asked me whether in these circumstances I would prefer to die immediately, I should certainly answer yes'.[13]

In fact, the famous lawyer was not empathising at all, but transferring his own adult mindset to those he spoke of, yet they would always see life very differently. He was unconsciously using the face-value judgment of a young child, all too common an error when supposedly intelligent minds consider differences that they find unacceptable. To love even our smallest neighbours as we love ourselves is to learn to think through *their* minds. Even newborn babies quickly show responsive appreciation of love, so this should be a significant consideration when discussing their best interests.

Uniquely valuable whatever the quality

Debates about the best use of medical resources increasingly hang on what is deemed (by others) to be a life of such poor quality that it should not be sustained. The use of the word 'it' should at once alert us to the total objectivity being used; we are dealing with people, not objects. Many who survive with severely challenged abilities still value their lives and have valid contributions to make on behalf of the rest of us. We only have to think of Stephen Hawking, with his huge neuromuscular problems, who still wrote the best seller, *A Brief History of Time,* amongst other literature.[14] Some might once have argued that the quality of his life must be so poor that it would not be cost-effective to invest vast resources in keeping him alive. Yet his brilliant contributions to scientific thought indicate that whatever the quality, his life has been of great value, both to himself and to others. Quality should never be confused with value, but it often is.

Someone might say, 'Ah yes, but Hawking's contributions have been intellectual, whereas some disabled babies will have such impaired intelligence that they will use up lots of vital resources without giving anything back'. Again, this is to use the face-value judgment so prevalent today. It is easy enough to bandy about stories of broken marriages and unhappy adolescents (by no means confined to disabled families), or to tot up the cost of the probable need for child protection and special education. Speculation is not evidence, and individual histories and controlled studies suggest that families with an incapacitated member often have a greater cohesion than average, which is in itself a social contribution.[15]

The cost-effectiveness of love

I was once deeply impressed by a mother's comment about her child, who could well have been put into the category despised by intellectuals and economists alike as a 'non-contributor'. But my commission from his mother was, 'Tell them that he's brought a lot of love'. Love is the most cost-effective resource we have, for it grows as it is given away and is usually returned with interest.

For those with ears to hear and eyes to see, there are similarly important messages to be pointed out to those whose judgment is swayed by appearances. A boy with Down's syndrome had three sisters, all of whom went into the caring professions. Two severely disabled children who only lived for a few years produced a growth spurt in the maturity of their mother and father. Neither child could ever speak, sit up or do much more than laugh and convulse, but the laughter was often generated by interplay with their loving parents. Amongst the family's friends were two with a strained marriage and two or three with addictions, but all took note and changed their ways. How much value was all that to society? It is hard to quantify the hidden value of two way love, or to find weight for it in economic debates.

Dangerous denial

The other factor playing a big but unrecognised part in some of these debates is an emotional one. The first reaction to any crisis of expectation is usually the 'Oh, no!' of denial, be it about the birth of a child with obvious disability or the prolonged dying of someone older. In suggesting that a quick end would be more merciful, philosophers think that they are treating these issues completely rationally but, like it or not, they cannot arrive at their conclusions from disembodied reason alone. As with the rest of us, their judgment can be subtly influenced by emotion, even when they deny the very denial itself.

Doctors, judges, economists and even parents can be influenced by current philosophical arguments to end it all as these are used to reinforce their own initially negative reactions, but then grief usually moves on. Families are those most likely to go on to suffer guilt, anger or depression should a decision have been taken to put an end to a beloved but afflicted life, but by then they are lost from centre stage.

Death denial can also be working overtime in those who insist that every possible medical or surgical means must be employed to protract life, even when it is clear from the start that this would be a futile exercise. Franco, Tito, Idi Amin and other heads of state have been put through this, no doubt largely for political reasons, but many less public figures suffer this way too. That this is not always the wisest use of resources should often be clear enough, but a sense of failure and the fear of litigation can bring death on a ventilator to some who would have fared better to die in the arms of loved ones.

We know from experience and example that believing prayer undoubtedly changes things, but I dare to whisper that some appeals to faith healers are also denying reality and generating false hope rather than encouraging genuine trust in our all-wise as well as all-powerful God. We fully affirm his omnipotence whilst believing that he knows best.

An anointed third way

The rights lobbies ('right to live' or 'right to die') need to be convinced of a third way. Palliative care and terminal relief can be given to babies and older folk alike, but hospice teams do not have the strident voices of most pro-life and pro-euthanasia enthusiasts. Again, this is an area where the heads of good Christian people need to be anointed afresh as they apply their minds to the best way of loving God and honouring his image in the weakest and most vulnerable of their neighbours, from first cry to last breath.

There are concentric rings of potential carers around every sick person, and whether these are immediately personal, medically professional or, as remoter resorts, legal and political, there is a great need for attentive listening and mutual understanding between them all. Many at the centre of the circle have testified to the way such pastoral care can transform a frighteningly bleak situation into one where relationships have been deepened, and the one at the heart of it all helped to face a more peaceful end.

The cross as the key to conflict resolution

Although I have dwelt on a few of the life and death dilemmas of medical practice, and more of these are regularly emerging, workers in other disciplines must also meet with clashes of opinion. In resolving these we need to take as our model the way that a just but loving God reconciled two seemingly opposite aspects of his character (the tension between Lord and Shepherd). Yes, the disobedience of humanity puts up a sin barricade and deserves the death penalty. Yet this grieves the merciful heart of our Creator, whose original design was for us to be in his image. The dilemma was once and for all resolved in the cross of Christ, as he took upon himself our death sentence, bridging the gap between God and man and offering a creative relationship instead of death and destruction.

The upright stake of the cross speaks of the descent of love incarnate, God made man in Jesus, the Christ. The horizontal represents his arms outstretched in reconciling forgiveness and, across the two, God in Christ paid the death penalty to conquer universal and personal evil on our behalf. We cannot imagine how much this cost Father and Son, but the Son's triumphant cry, 'It is finished', was followed by his resurrection, and then his return to the right hand of God. His costly commitment to creative relationship had been effective, and his revitalising Holy Spirit is now offered to those who turn to him for forgiveness and the eventual restoration of our lost imagery.

Martin Luther, founding father of the sixteenth century Reformation in Europe, had to deal with those who acted out their own faulty vision and inspiration by using extreme and violent methods for, as they saw it, purifying the church's life – loveless legalism at its worst and so much at odds with the divine pattern. His response to them was precisely in terms of the givenness of the cross as the touchstone of Christian understanding: *Crux probat omnia*, all things are to be measured by the cross alone.[16]

Trying to think Christianly in resolving our contemporary perplexities should still involve the same godly blend of self-giving goodness and mercy. The attempt is likely to cause what some (including John Stott) have called a 'pain in the mind' as we struggle to resolve the tension of two strong arguments that, as with our notions of justice and mercy, seem so often to pull in opposite directions. Yet the third person of the Trinity is there to help us.

Costly commitment to creative relationships

The cross of Christ is the pattern whereby we might draw two disparate factions together as our lives cross-connect in love with our righteous God and with our troubled (perhaps troublesome) neighbours and their knotty problems. Commitment to such connection is costly.

Yet in its practice we can be privileged to find the mediation of his Holy Spirit, who (as with the cross and resurrection) is able to bring something good out of something apparently bad. He still causes righteousness to triumph. We need to stay alert and responsive to that Spirit, for he promises to direct and enable us – to anoint our heads – as we seek for wisdom in channelling his self-giving love into new and different trouble spots. The eventual resolution of so many dilemmas is often relational as much as intellectual.*

Mediaeval stained glass windows or books of art sometimes show scenes of learned persons who are obviously discussing matters of great moment. Some have scientific instruments in their hands and it is evident that they are all thinking very hard. Hovering over their heads is the picture of a dove, often used to indicate the Holy Spirit of God. Not only in those days, many brilliant thinkers still acknowledge that, with his anointing, they have been helped to think God's thoughts after him. Through his grace, the same can be true of us lesser mortals.

---

* Professor John Wyatt competently enlarges this very sketchy discussion in his book *Matters of Life and Death*.[17] See also Alan and Paul Johnson's book *Making Sense of Medical Ethics*.[18] Those whose concerns lie in different arenas might find helpful the broader topics covered by Schluter and Lee in their publication *The R Option: Building Relationships as a Better Way of Life*.[19]

1 1 Samuel 16:11-13
2 Luke 7:44-46
3 James 3:6
4 Matthew 15:18-20
5 Philippians 4:7
6 2 Corinthians 1:21,22
7 Galatians 5:22,23
8 1 Corinthians 2:12-16
9 Matthew 22:37,38
10 John 7:24
11 Ephesians 4:14
12 Ephesians 4:15,16
13 *New Law Journal* 1981; 131:1040.
14 Hawking S. *A Brief History of Time: From the Big Bang to Black Holes.* New York: Bantam Books, 1995
15 Goodall J. *Disabled lives in a cost-conscious society.* University of Keele: MA thesis, 1991.
16 Williams R. *The wound of knowledge (second edition).* London: Darton, Longman and Todd, 1990.
17 Wyatt J. *Matters of Life and Death.* Leicester: Inter-Varsity Press, 1998.
18 Johnson AG, Johnson PR. *Making Sense of Medical Ethics: a hands-on guide.* London: Hodder Arnold, 2006.
19 Schluter M, Lee DJ. *The R Option: Building Relationships as a Better Way of Life.* Cambridge: The Relationships Foundation, 2002.

15

My cup overflows

In context, these words speak of overflowing contentment. We can almost see the lambs jumping about, wagging their tails with the joy of living, whilst the ewes look on benignly from their comfortable resting places. The valley is far behind, present dangers are being kept at bay, wounds soothed and all wants supplied. The shepherd has provided more than enough for every need and promises to keep it that way. The cup of life is indeed full to overflowing.

Cups of many kinds

Tracing biblical references to cups makes an interesting study. In the Old Testament, our modern slogan 'Think before you drink' is anticipated[1] but other writers give dire warnings about the cup of God's wrath, to be poured forth in judgment on disobedient people and nations.[2] In contrast, we can almost hear the psalmist, his sins forgiven, saying 'Cheers!' as he thankfully raises to God 'the cup of salvation'.[3] In the New Testament, most references are to the Lord's cup of suffering. What this contained is made clear in the Bible's last reference to a cup, golden on the outside but inside filled with abominable and filthy things. Resistant to being healed, the one who was trying to get others to drink would be wiped out.[4]

Yet it was the drinking of this kind of cup that Jesus faced in Gethsemane and, although revolted by it, he agreed to take it.[5] In doing so, he accepted the deadly consequences that should have been ours, something for which we give thanks when we share in communion with him and each other at his table. 'Is not the cup of thanksgiving for which we give thanks a participation in the blood of Christ?'[6] Someone who had led a dissolute life, but then came to see this truth, did actually say 'Cheers!' as he took the cup from the hands of the minister – his interpretation of 'Amen'. The glad response of our own hearts should cause our cups of salvation to overflow in thanksgiving. As Jesus reminded the Pharisees, it is not the outside appearance of a cup that matters, but what it holds inside.[7]

Full and running over

For a cup to run over, it is either being filled so fast that the contents spill over or it was full to the brim and has been jolted. Years ago, I saw Paul Brand illustrate this in practice. As a famous leprosy surgeon, he must have had patients whose thankfulness to him for successful complex surgery must often have bubbled over, but on that occasion his message was not at all complicated. He was speaking from a platform at a public meeting, the table supplied with the customary jug of water and a glass. He first filled the tumbler to the brim then, as he walked across the stage, simulated an accidental stumble. Of course, the water immediately overflowed. He then compared the tumbler to a Christian, and the water to whatever is filling that Christian's heart and mind, only made clear to others when the 'glass' is jolted or jostled. If we are filled with self-importance or self-pity, irritable words and behaviour or a stream of grievances will spill out. If, however, we are regularly anointed by the Holy Spirit of God for cleansing, soothing, renewing and refilling, then what overflows will reflect that, and can have an incalculable effect on those around us.

Years later at another conference in another country, a different surgeon, Alan Johnson, was speaking on Christian medical ethics. It was before the days of PowerPoint presentations and his talk was illustrated with transparencies projected onto a screen. Unfortunately, despite careful rehearsal, the projectionist made a hash of the presentation. Many illustrations were slow to appear, had to be reversed, or put the right way up – the stuff of a speaker's bad dreams. The subject matter was particularly important to the audience of nearly 2,000 people, representing many different countries and who in fact still listened well.

Afterwards, Alan was sadly disappointed that, to his mind, things had gone so badly, although at the time he had stayed calm and exhibited great patience with each new frustration. Hoping to be of some consolation to him, someone said, 'Alan, many of the folk in that audience would be used to their surgeons shouting and swearing or throwing instruments about the operating theatre when things went wrong. How you coped so calmly under stress would speak as loudly as what you'd hoped to get across by the talk itself'. The overflow had revealed telling evidence of a life filled with the Holy Spirit, the inspiration of the ethics.

As Jesus had foretold and as we have considered before, 'streams of living water' will flow from within a person who believes in him. To make the meaning quite clear, John added that by water he meant the Spirit.[8] As with the longsuffering surgeon, we are likely to be oblivious to the effect of this overflow, but the cup will need to be constantly replenished if we are to keep on acting as irrigation channels from our Lord to the barren and thirsty world about us. Our own spirits come alive when, in gratitude for his self-giving, we give ourselves to him and ask the resurrected Christ to live in us. He does this through his Spirit, and we can't have one without the other.[9]

Polluting, then purifying the stream

We can grieve the Spirit of God by letting self-centredness contaminate the overflow when we are jostled, producing a bitter, angry and malicious mixture instead of the purity of a kind, compassionate and forgiving output he would have inspired.[10] We therefore need to keep in step with the Spirit to be close enough for his 'sprinkler' to keep our spirits from getting dry. Much as a child longs to take the giant strides of a parent, so our goal is to match our steps to his. He helps us to grow up in order to produce his good fruit, not the bad fruit of our old self-centred nature.[11] As with the child, though, growth takes time.

The body of the church universal has sometimes overlooked the quiet, personal and productive presence in a life of the Holy Spirit, the third member of the Trinity. Yet how can a body, or its members, survive without a regular infusion of the water of life? Whereas the apostles experienced the Spirit's arrival as a dramatic event of infilling[12] and some believers still speak of memorable experiences, the testimony of most latter-day disciples is of being renewed day by day. The Spirit nudges us when we grieve him, reminding of the need to confess, to be cleansed and refilled. When the nudge has been resisted for a time, spiritual vitality is lowered, but eventual refilling can be accompanied by an obvious overflow of relief and joy.

On the lookout for drought

Existing personality traits and our state of physical health no doubt influence both how we feel and how much of that shows, but the Spirit of the Lord looks on the heart. He always longs to anoint afresh with the oil of gladness and restore praise, 'instead of a heavy burdened, and failing spirit....'[13]

Our cups can run low when the pressures of a busy life have squeezed out quiet times for enjoying the Shepherd's company, feeding on his Word, listening to his voice and making our lives available to him through prayer and supplication. As Nehemiah tells us, SOS prayers, offered in a crisis or when time is genuinely not our own, can be wonderfully answered.[14] To read the rest of his book is to realise that communion with God was an on-going aspect of Nehemiah's working life, as ideally it should be for all of us whatever our allotted task.

Another impressive point in his story is how, once Nehemiah had set his hand to the mighty task of rebuilding Jerusalem, the builders were made up of all ranks. They included the high priest himself, a goldsmith and a perfume maker – unlikely labourers, but prepared to knuckle down and help. Notable exceptions were the nobles of Tekoa, unwilling to take orders and refusing to put their superior shoulders to the work.[15] How chastened they might have been to find that a simple shepherd from their home town had already written the book of Amos, named after him, in which he had warned people such as themselves against complacency and pride. We are still reading his book centuries later, but all we can be sure about them is their uncooperative snobbishness.

The rich get richer as the poor get poorer

The same men of Tekoa were probably amongst the nobles later exposed by Nehemiah because out of their wealth they had lent money to the poor at such a crippling rate of interest that the people were starving.[16]

Does that have a familiar ring to it? The rich nations of the world have kept on doing the much same thing right up to the present day. Despite the surges of charitable giving that follow haunting television documentaries of people of all ages dying before our eyes, regular and sustained sharing is left to the few. There is no comparison between the lifestyle of most people in western society and those in impoverished countries, although admittedly some of their own 'nobles' still carry out the practices of 400 BC, making the poor poorer, when any accumulated wealth should spill over into meeting the needs of others. Sadly, western cups have sometimes run over with supplies of drugs and alcohol, the craving for which has ruined so many lives, from North American Indians to Australian aborigines, and countless others in between.

Experts in climate change believe that the extravagant use of fuel by the rich countries is largely responsible for global warming, whose effect contributes greatly to the drought and disease hitting poorer nations in particular. It will take more sacrifices than a few financial handouts to solve that inequality. Yet all over the world, those who follow the Shepherd are following one who released his right to a heavenly home for birth in a stable. As man he deemed service more desirable than status. His self-giving extended to the sacrifice of his life in order to save others. He graciously became poor so that we might become rich – rich in spiritual blessings and in the grace of giving.

As he wrote about this, Paul commended the rich generosity shown by people who were not well off financially but, having given themselves first to the Lord, were moved to give more than they could readily afford to help other believers in trouble.[17] The overflow of their cups in practical ways was a demonstration of the transformed outlook that should set the Shepherd's flock apart from the get-rich-quick attitude of much of the world, an attitude easily picked up by the unwary. Although the Spirit of the Lord has good news for the poor, the imprisoned and oppressed, the disabled and broken-hearted, and also offers comfort to those who mourn[18] the implications of that message continually need to register in Christian minds. Hands should reach into Christian pockets and sleeves be rolled up on Christian arms to relieve such suffering, both at home and abroad.

The treasurer of a Christian fellowship was once burdened about a great opportunity his organisation had for opening up fresh areas of witness and service. As ever, the problem was how to finance it all and he started to pray fervently for the funds to come in. The body that he represented was quite well to do, and as he prayed he sensed that the Lord was saying, 'Get up! I've already given them a lot of money'. His preferred task was to ask the membership to give a greater share of what they had already received rather than asking the Lord to shower down more. We have as inspiration his own generous giving, the scars on his hands, feet and brow and through his heart testifying to the price he was ready to pay for all now freely offered to us. He has given us all things richly to enjoy. Can we be less generous? It is easy enough to join in singing 'I surrender all', with great fervour and intellectual assent, but it is not so easy to do.

AW Tozer presents this challenge in a chapter entitled *The blessedness of possessing nothing*.[19] He takes Abraham's willingness to offer up Isaac as an example of complete obedience to God's call to surrender what he held most dear, and the blessing that then followed as he recognised that his real treasures were inward and eternal. Tozer warns, 'There can be no doubt that this possessive clinging to things is one of the most harmful habits in life. Because it is so natural, it is rarely recognized for the evil that it is. But its outworkings are tragic…Everything is safe which we commit to Him, and nothing is really safe which is not so committed'. Further, 'We will be brought one by one to the testing place, and we may never know when we are there. At that testing place there will be no dozen possible choices for us – just one and an alternative – but our whole future will be conditioned by the choice we make'.

Living more simply so that others may simply live

Remembering how much he lowered his standard of living for our sakes, we must each prayerfully decide what sort of lifestyle will honour our Lord the most. We can so easily make others covetous by having too grand a house (inside and outside), too gas-guzzling a car, too lavish a wardrobe or just too many possessions. Are they clutched in tight fists or held in open hands? Jesus warned us not to hold on to such things but, in learning to put his kingdom first, we find instead that he provides all that we truly need.[20] He richly provides us with everything for our enjoyment – a statement Paul made to Timothy in the context of his exhorting the wealthy to share.[21]

Remembering that one in six of the world's population lives on less than one US dollar a day is an incentive to spend less on self and to share with others, especially if we reclaim and add income tax through Gift Aid in the UK. Gifts can be channelled through agencies known to be honourable, giving priority to those who hope to further the kingdom of God. For some, total self-giving might involve changing countries and cultures, but systematically to support and pray for individual care workers and teachers, our representatives as well as his, will be more effective than scattering gifts impulsively and indiscriminately. Backing agencies that work with indigenous churches can help to transform the lives of people in poor communities, teaching methods of self-help bringing a boost to their self-worth.

Deluded or delighted?

Today as I write, two moving stories have been in the news. One gave a glimpse of many smart new residences going up in the home town of some less prosperous Chinese men. They had borrowed vast sums of money to go abroad, hoping after many years to earn enough to build similar houses. Yet over 20 of them have been drowned in the course of their hard labour of cockle picking. We cannot blame these men for wanting to improve their lot but the grasping gang master, having sold for huge profit what he had gained for a pittance, was justifiably sentenced to long years of imprisonment for their manslaughter.

One of the widows was interviewed. She had been left with huge debts and would far rather have her husband home and alive than to have the more comfortable life he had died for. Their hoped for gain had become a dead loss, and her cup overflowed with sorrow, bitterness and fear for the future.

The other story was of the liberation, after months of captivity, of an elderly hostage and his companions, held to ransom by their foreign kidnappers. Although accused by many of naivety, they had gone to that country at their own expense to share the peace and the love of God, aware that other costs might be asked of them. At intervals the strain of captivity had shown in their videoed faces as they were forced to repeat to the world their captors' demands; viewers feared for their lives. One was indeed killed, but the others were freed. Prepared to die, they had been granted life.

The cups of the reunited families overflow with relief, gratitude and gladness. Yet at times the oldest of the captives admitted that his cup had been emptied of all that. We are not exempt from sharing the Lord's cup of suffering, for when he said 'Follow me' he was on the way to the cross. We need to take time, thinking and thanking, for the cup of gratitude to be replenished and then to run over.

Precious to God

Friends of mine, Dick and Sarah, had two profoundly disabled children who both died but with whom they had known much joy as well as pain. Sarah wrote a book, *Precious to God*,[22] about their lives. Although the couple were abstemious in their tastes, they had learned from the experience with and through their children that relationships were more precious than gold. When later they were blessed by the arrival of Alice, they brought her up to share these same values.

Like many little girls, when Alice was about nine she decided that shopkeeping would be fun, so she set out her stall of small, unwanted treasures and invited her school friends, preferably with their parents, to come and buy. Amazingly, her takings amounted to a larger sum than she had ever possessed before. When asked what she was going to do with it though, she immediately replied, 'Why! I'm going to give it to someone who needs it'. This she did, selecting as recipient the special school attended years earlier by the sister she had never met. The staff's warm reception and gratitude, and their memories of her sister, meant more to her than anything bought just for herself could have done. Little wonder that her mother's book ends by giving thanks to God for her, adding 'and my cup overflows'. More valleys would lie ahead, but any who hold out a hand of faith to the Shepherd, even in the dark, will always find it held. As the comfort of his love is on offer for all, those already comforted will long to share such rich generosity with 'someone who needs it'.

For most of us, the theory might be fine, but the practical outworking can be harder. That is why the Shepherd puts us into flocks, to encourage one another.[23] Even the lambs can have something to teach the rest of us.

1 Proverbs 23:29-35
2 Jeremiah 25:15-29
3 Psalm 116:12,13
4 Jeremiah 51:7-9; Revelation 17:4-6
5 Luke 22:42
6 1 Corinthians 10:16
7 Matthew 23:25,26
8 John 7:37-39
9 Romans 8:9-11
10 Ephesians 4:29-32
11 Galatians 5:16-26
12 Acts 2:1-4
13 Isaiah 61:3 (Amplified Bible)
14 Nehemiah 2:1-6
15 Nehemiah 3:5
16 Nehemiah 5:7
17 2 Corinthians 8:1-5
18 Isaiah 61:1-3; Luke 4:18,19
19 Tozer AW. *The Pursuit of God.* Carlisle: Authentic Lifestyle, 2005 (originally published 1948).
20 Matthew 6:19-34
21 1 Timothy 6:17-19
22 Bowen S. *Precious to God.* Crowborough: Christina Press, 1997.
23 Hebrews 10:25

16

Goodness and mercy will follow me....

Modern translations replace the older 'goodness and mercy' with 'goodness and love', though today love is a much abused word and lacks mercy's hint of clemency. Loving kindness might be better, but we'll stick to mercy here. Once again, with the pairing of goodness and mercy, David reminds us of the complementary activities of his Lord and Shepherd: the two arms of authority and care; the interplay of righteousness and restoration; and the exercise, when necessary, of a corrective rod and comforting staff. Now soothed, satisfied and comfortably oiled, the sheep have to get up and go on. The Shepherd's *leading* continues, but with emphasis now on the tokens of his presence *following*.

The psalms are full of references to God's goodness. He is good to all; he has compassion on all he has made.[1] God alone is completely good[2] and is offended by evil.[3] On the other hand, he is also self-giving love personified.[4] We have here another perfect balance: the purity of divine goodness met by the generosity of divine mercy towards those who would otherwise merit a sterner judgment. Once more we can marvel how goodness and mercy came together in the person of the one accurately known as the *Good* Shepherd, who gave his life for the sheep. Made like us, he became a *merciful* high priest and made atonement for our sins.[5] He who knew no sin was made sin for us, so that in him we might become the righteousness of God.[6]

Sheepdog trials
My father used to refer to the two qualities of goodness and mercy as the heavenly sheepdogs, working with their Shepherd to keep his sheep on the right track. Should any have erred and strayed from his ways, got lost, or simply should he want to change their direction, then the sheepdogs spring into action. *Goodness* steers errant sheep

back towards the paths of righteousness, whilst *merciful love* comes up on the other side, gently guiding them away from possible bypaths. Two dogs work together with the common purpose of bringing the wanderers back within range of their shepherd's voice and in reach of his staff. Peter might equally have called church elders sheepdogs when he referred to them as overseers. He makes it clear that their role was to be one of service, not superiority, as they kept their flock on course.[7]

David's experience had included at least one landmark lesson in finding how goodness and mercy worked together to keep him on the paths of righteousness. In 1 Samuel, we are given a lovely account of how the goodness of Abigail persuaded David to have mercy on her husband, the man who had so insulted him that David planned to put him and his people to the sword.[8] This would have been the expected reaction in the contemporary culture, but Abigail clearly saw that as a result David would bear 'the staggering burden of needless bloodshed' and dissuaded him from such precipitate action. Hearing of his reprieve seems to have given drunken Nabal a heart attack from which he died. If David's earlier plan had gone ahead, Abigail would have died in the intended slaughter. As it was, he later married her.

A shepherd needs under-shepherds

Two experienced shepherds have written about their personal experiences of training reliable working dogs, Phillip Keller in his *Lessons from a Sheepdog*[9] and David Kennard in a beautifully illustrated volume *A Shepherd's Watch: Through the Seasons with One Man and his Dogs*.[10] Keller describes his working dog, Lass, as a kind of under-shepherd, and each author indicates very clearly how much a shepherd relies on good and faithful dogs, quickly responsive to every signal and becoming extensions of the shepherd's own arms.

David Kennard describes how he and his dog Swift rescued a frightened lamb from a cliff face after a visitor's dog, out of control, had chased it there. Like sheepdog trials, such exercises illustrate the beautiful harmony between dogs and shepherd as they work together to gather and direct the flock. This only happens after long hours of training. Similarly our Shepherd's under-shepherds, his pastors, need to be trained.

Phillip Keller drew telling spiritual parallels from the way he trained Lass. When he took over her care, she was a wild, snarling, shackled and abused creature, tied up in a city backyard. Even after he had freed and fed her, she remained hostile. He had almost given up hope of ever gaining her trust when, standing gazing into the sunset one evening, he felt a muzzle in his hand. His loving care had overcome the fear that had made the animal hostile and he could now start teaching her how to co-operate. As she gradually learned complete trust and obedience, she also discovered that this was the life she was made for, and became one of his best sheepdogs. Keller compares all this with God's dealings towards us as we have similar lessons and gradually learn the satisfaction of teaming up with our Shepherd.

Training can be tough

It is an interesting study to see training in leadership at work in Peter the fisherman. Called from his nets to follow Jesus, he had learned the hard way what a changed lifestyle his obedience involved. Like Paul, he must often have said, 'When I want to do good, evil is right there with me'.[11] Although desirous of following his Shepherd he repeatedly failed; but as we have already read, he was drawn back by love and mercy.[12] Jesus did not cast him off but promoted him to feed sheep instead of catching fish! He was to exchange his struggles and setbacks for spiritual shepherding, a calling dramatically confirmed after the coming of the Holy Spirit into his life.

Only then do we find him addressing crowds and drawing in thousands of new believers. He had become under-shepherd to the Good Shepherd, trained by his earlier experiences. Even his failures gave him more understanding, not only of his own weak points but towards those of others as well. Then, after years of being a front runner, he had to take a back seat whilst Paul steamed ahead, leaving Peter to share his hard-won lessons on humility with the next generation.[13] The Shepherd's training never ends.

As was always the case with Peter, love of the Shepherd might for any of us involve daunting possibilities. Readiness to obey grows with each experience of his goodness and love. Even when Lass came back scratched and bleeding after searching for a sheep lost in the undergrowth, Keller describes their mutual pleasure as the task was accomplished. Her suffering came second to the satisfaction of having done his will and received his 'Well done!'

Many of today's under-shepherds, and often their flocks, endure great suffering for their faithfulness to the Lord Jesus Christ. Prisoners of conscience are usually the victims of misplaced zeal, the pursuit of what is thought good by their persecutors neglecting the complementary need for mercy towards those with a different allegiance. To those imprisoned for their faith, sometimes under sentence of death, the Shepherd has a way of making his goodness and loving kindness known, perhaps in some small way that in brighter days might not have registered. A loving letter or postcard can speak volumes when most other communication is harsh. As gently as a dog might lick our fingers as we walk along, so lightly might such reassurances convey the Shepherd's continuing concern. Seeing this, fellow prisoners and even captors have sometimes turned to him, discovering a freedom of spirit unknown before.

Too strict or too soft?

Serious risks for many are either that being over judgmental can masquerade as 'goodness', or that simply being kind hearted can be deemed 'merciful'. When no clear principle is at stake, the Shepherd's under-shepherds must be especially careful to set a good example to their charges, neither laying down the law about non-essentials nor letting licence go unchecked. The Shepherd's intention is that under-shepherds will work in close harmony with him, learning to find the balance between legalism and liberalism, authority and humility, goodness and mercy. 'It is fine to be zealous, provided the purpose is good', said Paul.[14] The hallmarks of our behaviour should be love for God and neighbour, but our problems often arise within the detail. Whereas God has provided us with everything for our enjoyment[15] another of Paul's sayings applies: 'Each one should be fully convinced in his own mind' about what is permissible in given circumstances.[16]

Peter illustrated this very clearly in his address and testimony to the council of Jerusalem.[17] It was not lack of principle on his part that had waived the need of circumcision for Gentile believers, but he had seen for himself that God's instant gift of the Holy Spirit to them indicated their acceptance within the fold without the need for the rites of the Old Covenant. They had heard the good news of the death and resurrection of the Lamb of God and trusted him for their salvation. That was enough to bring about their New Covenant relationship and Peter's revised opinion, through which they would now be included in fellowship.

Come what may, his goodness and mercy never fail

It was the hostility of his brothers that had catapulted Joseph into the ordeal of trudging along the tortuous road that finally led to his premiership. Yet in the end, full of grace and mercy, he told them, 'You intended to harm me, but God intended it for good'.[18] In another wonderful passage about the good purposes of God, Paul described in detail some of the hardships that can (and do) face those who have responded to his love. Even when considered 'as sheep to be slaughtered', *nothing at all* can separate us from the love of Christ. 'No, in all these things we are more than conquerors through him who loved us.'[19] There must have been many times for both Joseph and Paul when it was tempting to see things differently, but the heavenly sheepdogs had finally directed them to the places appointed for them from the beginning. When we are tempted to doubt God's goodness, then is the time to cling to the promise of his merciful love and later to look back, not in anger but in amazement.

Following faithfully to the end

Just as his goodness and mercy follow us throughout our lives, temporal and eternal, we too should leave a trail of these qualities behind us – the overflow from the cup – both in the way we live and how we face death. Our early years can be marked by lapses in trust and obedience, and the middle years are notorious for slackened enthusiasm, or wandering into bypaths found easier underfoot. When 'all the days' of life have almost gone, how good it would be to be leaving behind the final legacy of good and merciful lives that have brought glory to God. This will mean faithful following and endurance day by day, to the end of the track.

To look ahead and see the Shepherd's wounds, to spend time hearing and responding to his call and to look around in gratitude at so many tokens of his goodness and mercy: these cannot fail to encourage us, each and all, to act in responsive love as we keep on keeping on whilst helping others to do the same – until at last we encounter the Chief Shepherd.[20]

Recently I listened to a broadcast service from the Liverpool church previously attended by a black teenager, Anthony Walker, who was stabbed to death in a racially motivated attack without any provocation on his part. At the time there was a national outcry, and both then and in the service his mother spoke movingly of how she had always taught her children that they must daily look for things to forgive. Through the mediation of Jesus, God had forgiven them, so how could she withhold the offer of forgiveness from the murderers of her beloved son? She hoped one day to meet them and tell them so. Her under-shepherding had been both good and merciful and inspired many others. We heard of many wonderful things that happened in the wake of this public witness to the love, mercy and power of God as he upheld his children in and beyond their valley – a lovely reminder of how the darkness of Good Friday paved the way for the glory of Easter Sunday.

Despite her grief, that mother might well have echoed the words of the hard-pressed Jeremiah, 'I have not run away from being your shepherd' – or even from being your sheepdog.[21]

1   Psalm 145:9
2   Matthew 19:17
3   Habakkuk 1:13
4   1 John 4:8
5   Hebrews 2:17
6   2 Corinthians 5:21
7   1 Peter 5:1-4
8   1 Samuel 25
9   Keller P. *Lessons from a Sheepdog.* London: Hodder and Stoughton, 1984.
10 Kennard D. A *Shepherd's Watch: Through the Seasons with One Man and his Dogs.* London: Headline Book Publishing, 2004.
11 Romans 7:21
12 John 21
13 1 Peter 5:5,6
14 Galatians 4:18
15 1 Timothy 6:17
16 Romans 14:5
17 Acts 15:5-11
18 Genesis 50:20
19 Romans 8:28-39
20 1 Peter 5:2-6
21 Jeremiah 17:16

17

…all the days of my life

As the days of our lives proceed, the natural expectation is that childhood will lead to adulthood and the middle years to ripe old age. Death is what happens to other people, but it shocks us when some of those others die young. Failing powers will come as a surprise to those who have not allowed the implications of their birth certificates to make them face facts.

We have implied from David's psalm that we might not only expect the Shepherd to pursue us with goodness and mercy to the end of our lives, but that in our more mature years these qualities will overflow from our full cups to bless others. The psalm itself reveals something of how his varied experiences of God's care had helped David to become a blessing to us. Spiritual maturity is something all Christians are called to aspire to and although it is unlikely that David would have been charting his own spiritual growth he might have enjoyed pausing to graze with us amongst some of today's fresher insights.

Growing up
Whereas Jesus said that we must become like little children in order to enter his kingdom, and that humility should remain a hallmark of our allegiance to him,[1] the Good Shepherd still expects his lambs to grow up into sheep![2] This takes time and, just as a child proceeds through various conceptual milestones to reach adult thought, it is interesting (at least to a paediatrician) to find suggestions in the Bible that a parallel pattern might be followed as we grow up spiritually.

Spiritual and intellectual maturity are not the same
This suggested sequence does not at all mean that I am trying to equate spiritual maturity with high intelligence, but simply suggesting a similar developmental sequence for both. God still chooses the

foolish things of the world to shame the wise. Thus an eleven year old boy (with about half the IQ of that expected of him) once entered the consulting room and greeted me with 'Doctor, doctor, do you know that Christ died for our sins?' He began to repeat John chapter 3, verse 16 and was very happy when I joined in. Yet some of the world's honoured intellectuals are oblivious to the need for spiritual growth, denying the very existence of God. We *can* have one kind of wisdom without the other. In contrast, we are told that the child Jesus himself grew in wisdom as well as stature.[3] At his baptism when he was about 30 years old, the Spirit of God descended on and filled him as he received the Father's unreserved commendation.[4]

What, then, is this longed for spiritual maturity? Clearly, it must have to do with the indwelling of God's Holy Spirit in the life of a believer and depends on his wisdom at work and our cooperation, not on our own brilliance. New Testament writers hint about what this means, as well as describing some causes of arrested development. Epaphras was a faithful prayer supporter of the church at Colosse and prayed earnestly for its members to 'stand firm in all the will of God, mature and fully assured' whilst himself still looking for fruitfulness elsewhere.[5] Unshakeable faith in and obedience to God, based on his Word and attested by experience, with a life graced by the fruits and gifts of his Spirit, these are all characteristic of a spiritually mature believer in Christ.

Me, me, me

In contrast, the innate hallmark of infantile thought is egocentricity. Although responsive to loving attention, with growing attachment to those who give it, small children respond to inner discomforts and outer atmospherics with barometric swings of emotion. When urging the young Ephesian church to become mature, Paul particularly cited their need to stop being like infants, 'blown here and there by every wind of teaching'.[6] Each part of the body of Christ should not just do its own thing but learn to inter-relate and 'grow up into him who is the Head'.[7]

Growing up is a process, confirmed in Hebrews chapter six, verse one by the call to 'leave the elementary teachings about Christ and *go on* to maturity….' Paul distinguished between godly wisdom, revealed to the mature, and worldly wisdom, shortsighted and coming to nothing.[8] He told the young Christians in Corinth that they were still infantile[9] and, like those addressed by Peter, still needed basic baby food.[10] As physical growth starts by simply drinking milk, so to take in the 'milk of the word'[11] is the first step in spiritual development, perhaps as a response to the stories of Jesus and his love. Trying to digest the inner meaning of parables comes later.

Matching and mismatching

Basic to future growth in understanding is the ability to put like with like, whether using building blocks, colours or shapes. Matching words with appropriate people and objects is how language grows, but new ideas or experiences can be confusingly mismatched. Thus, the little boy found looking so terrified when the doctor returned to listen to his chest had thought he been out to get his 'deathoscope'. Another five year old arrived at an instant diagnosis when the storyteller told of the growing concern in the Bethany household when Lazarus fell ill and refused his dinner. Eyes sparkling with fellow feeling, he said, 'I know! He'd got the measles!' The teacher became uneasily aware that death and resurrection were likely to be tricky concepts to tackle with his age group.

A careful reading of Mark chapter four shows how the disciples did not see the inner meaning of the Parable of the Sower until Jesus carefully matched the sites onto which the seeds were falling with the diverse responses of those being offered God's Word. Unfamiliar words and ideas can baffle. I recall being mystified as a small child by the end of Mark chapter twelve where the Lord commended the widow who had cast her two 'mites' into the collecting box at the Temple.[12] My experience of Israeli coinage was nil and I only knew the word 'mite' as applied to small people like me. I accordingly thought to myself, 'Poor little children' – and was very relieved that she had given away 'all that she had', so there were no more left at home to suffer the same fate.

Those teaching Bible truths to young children therefore need to keep things simple and avoid words with double meanings. As with the disciples, matching new ideas to past experience gets the message across. A country child is more likely than a street urchin to grasp the idea of Jesus being like a shepherd, but a youthful TV addict might misinterpret 'taking Jesus into your heart' as an activity requiring open heart surgery.

Many who are new to faith can make similar errors because of language more familiar to insiders than to them. For some 'salvation' speaks of armies with brass bands, and 'redemption' applies to lottery tickets or pawnbrokers. Jesus' followers, though grown men, did not yet understand his double meaning when he referred to fermenting hostility as 'yeast'.[13] Confusions can be clarified better in smaller groups than in pews, hence the growing popularity of Alpha groups and the like.

Spiritual infants of any age have to learn right from wrong ('teaching about righteousness') but as they take in more solid food, by the constant use of God's Word, they will learn this and much more.[14] Yet the persistence of a mindset that judges by face-values sometimes leads to a literal interpretation of what others might perceive as biblical picture language, or the description of a long-discontinued custom. We can no doubt think up our own examples, but a text taken out of context can become a pretext for misguided teaching and practice.

Keeping up with the Joneses

The basic concept of matching, or of copying others, often lingers on into adult life as young – and not so young – parents try to keep up with the smart set. At the same time they can deprive their children of precious personal interaction and thereby provoke emotional disturbance. With rare insight, the mother of one such child said, 'We are so busy making him a good home that we are never in it'. Copying the Joneses had let her family down in the most important area of their lives – the intended image within them of a self-sacrificing God, for whom loving relationships always come first.

It might look the same but it isn't the same

As they learn that things are not always what they seem, even primary school children begin to see that lookalikes can mislead. There are toadstools as well as mushrooms and goats as well as sheep. Neither does a change of shape mean change of substance. Clay can be shaped into an attractive bowl but is still clay. People's skins or bodies might look different but they are still like us inside.

In his book *Simply Christian*, Tom Wright points out: 'the West' is in some minds equated with 'Christian', although 'most people in the Western world are not Christians and most Christians do not live in 'the West'.[15] Most actually live in Africa or South-East Asia'. The goods matter more than the label, but many African and Asian Christians have been shocked to sample the goods when moving to what they had thought was a Christian country. Just as it hurts when a small child's errors are laughed at, so growth in understanding is often painful. Misconceptions are clarified by experience as well as by kindly instruction from more mature minds.

Developing insight and judgment

Older primary school children are able to recognise that words can have more than one meaning, no longer fearful to stroke the cat 'because Granny died of a stroke'. This age group delights in puns and the jokes that employ them and, for the first time, can grasp the inner meaning of parables and proverbs. By now, they should start to perceive rather than judging by externals alone. Some could get the point of a poem posted outside the Memorial Chapel in Gloucester Cathedral. Referring to the treasured Colours of the Gloucestershire Regiment held there, it reads:

> A moth eaten rag on a worm eaten pole
> It does not look likely to stir a man's soul.
> 'Twas the deeds that were done 'neath the moth-eaten rag
> When the pole was a staff, and the rag was a flag.

Awareness of history and associations also makes a big difference to our perception of the worth of the frail and worn out who live (or die) amongst us. Quality is not a valid indicator of value. A child's prayer reveals this insight: 'Lord, please help us to see what people are like on the inside as well as looking at them on their outside'.

Weighing up pros and cons

By the time they enter secondary school, young minds should be growing in flexibility, taking the long view when weighing up alternatives and foreseeing consequences, instead of judging by appearances only or relying on preconceptions. Altruism develops, with its associated concepts of fairness, justice and the correction of inequalities – by goodness and mercy – along with youthful idealism and hero worship.

Although invisible and immeasurable, awareness of such abstract concepts has spiritual implications. Some who learn about him might now decide to follow the Shepherd, better able to realise the depth of his love and to weigh up what is, or might be, involved in commitment to him.

In the supposedly developed world, the dying and death of a young person is out of the natural order of things, yet can uncover the need for spiritual security. I think of eleven year old Anthony who, unlike the rest of his family, had always been interested in matters of faith. When told that his cancer was no longer responsive to treatment, he simply said, 'Well, my life is in God's hands. It's up to him what happens now'. On another occasion he said to his mother,

'You know, Mum, when I die you're not to get all upset. I'll be with Jesus. It's you left behind I feel sorry for'. Such were his faith and hope that his parents later came to share them.

Belief affects behaviour

As minds grow up, judgment should improve. Autonomy emerges, with partial awareness of its risk of autocracy as well as the benefit of free choice. It can be appreciated, though not always practised, that reconciliation would be a more mature response than sustained wrangling. There is a new perception of, if strong disagreement with, the viewpoints of others and partisanship grows between the like-minded. In secular culture this can encourage a gang mentality in place of friendship; in some Christian circles, cliques and controversy grow instead of unity.

Sometimes the vigour of a defensive reaction denotes consciousness of the humiliating void within. 'Why do you Christians believe that?' can be a serious, not a scoffing question. If the answer given is backed up by the life lived, the Holy Spirit often uses friendship or personal example as a doorway to faith.

Things seen and not seen

Instead of finding faith, the prevailing attitudes of culture or family too often take over the growing mind. Adolescents then become adults with the same materialistic and hedonistic priorities as prevail in much of the job market, despite giving occasional lip service to loftier concepts and ideals. Sadly, double standards for truth and justice are so much the cultural norm that older people beginning the Christian life often have much to unlearn, including a few past ideologies. The idea of humility as being Christ-like can be tough for a previous go-getter to accept and emulate.

As was touched on in chapter 14, even in ordinary professional or political life, and for obviously intelligent people, conceptual maturation can be arrested at the levels of egocentricity, face-value judgment or short-term planning. Important but intangible interpersonal assets are discounted in the materialistic reckoning of most balance sheets. Thus, hospital chaplains can be expected to monitor their efficiency by time and motion studies, and drinks machines replace office tea ladies. Whatever our walk in life, we are no doubt familiar with the impersonal atmosphere that such 'economies' bring with them, the image of God forgotten. Spiritual awakening can bring a belated, and often painful, shift in priorities. To try to sweeten relationships within the workplace is to oil its machinery – and will improve its output.

Keep on keeping on

Each Christian's goal should be to develop the mind of Christ, through his Spirit, and to reflect his glory, gradually being transformed into his likeness.[16] If maturity is to be measured by the fullness of Christ, then as Paul indicated, most of us still have a long way to go.[17] Perhaps it is easier to recognise the stage at which others have arrested than to scrutinise ourselves, but James reminds us that perseverance will be needed if we are to become 'mature and complete'. The comfort is that God offers the necessary wisdom to get us there.[18]

Just as healthy development from infancy to adolescence largely correlates with the loving interaction, support and tuition of those near and dear, so walking though life responsive to the directions of the Shepherd and keeping in step with his Spirit is to be on track towards spiritual maturity. Fellowship with others on the journey brings human encouragement. God has designed us for creative relationships, with him and with our fellow believers.

Developmental delay

So why do so many Christians lag behind in maturity, or stay forever babes in Christ? Some have not been well taught, but sometimes the egocentricity of immaturity chooses to ignore the Spirit's promptings. In the parable of the sower, Jesus also warns us that when life's worries, riches and pleasures choke the reception of his word, such people 'do not mature'. Mature lives, like mature trees, bear fruit and for this he said that we must hear the Word, retain it and, once again, persevere in the wisdom so gained.[19]

Every gardener knows that a single attack on weeds is not enough, but vigilance and perseverance are called for. The best weed killer for the spirit's choking thorns is the regular application of God's Word; Jesus said that this would bear maximum fruit in the receptive soil of a noble and good heart – one being taught by his Spirit. It is worth unpacking his words in more detail.

Worried?

Worries can start early. Some seem to be born with an anxious disposition, whilst others have been emotionally wounded in early life, sometimes by misconceptions harboured ever since. The cares of this life can indeed mount up but, instead of fixing our gaze on the one who endured so much for us and now longs to help and encourage us,[20] we glue our eyes to the problem. Sometimes we need someone wise in the wisdom of God to come alongside as a prayerful channel for the Spirit's healing ministry, to remind us from his Word that our Lord reigns over all. It really does iron out the worry lines to cast our burdens onto him.

Poor little rich folk

Contrary to the wisdom of the world, which views them as status symbols, Jesus identified the pursuit of riches and pleasures as barriers to spiritual maturity. By choking the appetite for his Word, they stop the intended harvest it would have produced. We have already deduced from the first verse of our psalm that to repeatedly say 'I want' is usually a mark of egocentric immaturity. Yet advertisers long to hear our 'Me too!' One agency even attempts to seduce buyers with the slogan, 'Me, me, me – and why not me?' Rather than saying 'I want', our deepest desire should be to find out what *he* wants, only to find ourselves overwhelmingly enriched as we walk in his ways and learn to share his gifts with others.

Listen and learn

As he ended the parable, Jesus said that to be 'good and noble' we should not just speed read his Word but listen attentively to it, retain it – hold it fast and remember it – and persevere in its application. As he spoke, the Holy Spirit had not yet fallen on his followers but the resultant abundant crop he referred to is readily identifiable in maturing believers as the fruit of his indwelling Spirit.

Perseverance is essential for maturity; yet ever since the days of the early church it has been so easy for Christians to drift into the easier path of conformity with the mindset and mores of this world, something Paul clearly warns us about.[21] At the end of his letter to the Colossians he adds greetings from Demas;[22] but later he reported sadly, 'Demas, because he loved this world, has deserted me'.[23] When the going had got tough for Paul, Demas opted for a more pleasurable life, and got going.

How did Jesus enjoy life?

Jesus, whilst warning about the harmful effects on fruitfulness of preoccupation with riches and pleasures, seems to have been without loose cash[24] and was of no fixed abode.[25] Yet he still lived life to the full. He enjoyed the pleasure of communion with his Father, of relieving the needs of others and, as he walked and talked with his friends, often enjoyed 'God's other book', from which (as in so many parables) he frequently drew lessons about God's tender loving care and our proper response to it.[26] He regularly attended a place of worship, and could also be the life and soul of a party. Although the gospellers mention only his weeping, he must have had a wonderful laugh. A walk in the country, spending time with other worshippers, or simply relaxing in good company can similarly restore our focus. These are healthier ways of strengthening relationships with family and friends than one shopping expedition too many.

A conference speaker once told his attentive audience that he had three important words to offer about the development of a fruitful Christian lifestyle. With all notebooks duly poised, he then said, 'Simplify, simplify, simplify!' The earthly life of our Good Shepherd certainly underlined that principle. The perfect example of spiritual maturity, he was singularly perceptive[27] and displayed all the qualities promised to us as the fruits of his Spirit when we abide in him. Paul lists these for us: love, joy, peace, patience, kindness, goodness, faithfulness, gentleness and self-control. [28] Jesus showed all these fruits in his early life and now longs to produce them in us.

Growing up to be like Jesus

In summary, the natural growth of human understanding proceeds from the egocentricity of infancy, through the misconceptions and malleability of early childhood, to the possibility of other-centred idealism in later life. Perception should slowly replace judgment by appearances, but developmental arrest can happen at any stage.

Spiritual maturity, becoming like Jesus, is a life-long process and only when we meet him will we be made like him. At the end of Paul's famous passage on 'the most excellent way', he summarises his own progress from reasoning like a child, then putting childish ways behind him and now approaching his longed for maturity. After practising so much intense hatred in earlier life, he had spent years learning to love and now foresaw the next stage when, as he said, 'I shall know fully, even as I am fully known'.[29] Until that happened, he knew that the goal he sought still lay ahead of him. Every one of us needs to echo his words: 'Not that I have already obtained all this, or have already been made perfect, but I press on to take hold of that for which Christ Jesus took hold of me...Only let us live up to what we have already attained'.[30]

To the end of our lives, there will always be more of his wisdom to learn, but when the Chief Shepherd returns we shall be caught up in the great wonder of resurrection, and at last become like him.[31] This hope should motivate us to grow up and get ready so that we may be unashamed before him at his coming.[32] If we are to hear his 'Well done, good and faithful servant', all the days of our lives should, at least from now on, be invested in what will best please and honour him, perhaps epitomised by sowing with and for him the seeds of his goodness and mercy in a world waxing weary of its own wild oats.[33]

1   Matthew 18:1-4
2   John 21:15-17
3   Luke 2:52
4   Luke 3:21-23
5   Colossians 4:12,13
6   Ephesians 4:14
7   Ephesians 4:13-15
8   1 Corinthians 2:4-10
9   1 Corinthians 3:1-4
10   1 Peter 2:2
11   1 Peter 2:2 (Authorised Version)
12   Mark 12:41-44 (Authorised Version)
13   Matthew 16:5-12
14   Hebrews 5:12-6:3
15   Wright T. *Simply Christian.* London: SPCK, 2006.
16   1 Corinthians 2:14-16; 2 Corinthians 3:17,18
17   Ephesians 4:13-15
18   James 1:4,5
19   Luke 8:14,15
20   Hebrews 12:2,3
21   Romans 12:2
22   Colossians 4:14
23   2 Timothy 4:10
24   Matthew 17:24-27
25   Luke 9:58
26   Matthew 6:25-34
27   Matthew 9:4
28   Galatians 5:22,23
29   1 Corinthians 13:11,12
30   Philippians 3:12-16
31   1 John 3:2
32   1 John 2:28
33   Matthew 25:14-23,40

18

I shall dwell in the house of the Lord....

David's own house was one he had been given by another king, Hiram. It was a beautiful palace made of finest cedar wood, no expense spared, but it suddenly and embarrassingly dawned on him that in contrast, the Ark of the Covenant was still housed in a tent. (The Ark was a very special portable box, and was the symbol of the Lord's abiding presence when his people obeyed him.) David had a great desire to build a worthier, more permanent 'house of the Lord'.[1] In the end, this task fell to his son Solomon, but David had drawn up the plans and perhaps dreamt of sometime, somehow being in that house with him. We cannot know whether or not his vision stretched to include a heavenly house, as ours now does, but his wording encourages us to look further than Solomon's Temple. We'll begin with earthly alternatives to the house David had in mind.

Houses of the Lord, great and small

Before building a house for the Lord, Solomon, too, had built an ambitiously grand palace for himself. It is easy to follow this example and serve our own interests before God's, putting mortgages before mission in our calculations. Yet having first decided what proportion of income will be specifically dedicated to him, some of us love to tell how his hand has been quietly at work, finding ideal but affordable homes. My own home falls into this category, but was found after viewing 189 others – a heart-sinking search that lasted for nearly two years! The perfect place finally surfaced only weeks after I'd arranged covenanted giving on the basis of my then current income exclusive of the anticipated cost of a house. The way things worked out involved a very modest outlay and I slowly arrived at a lesson about putting God's affairs first. Individual circumstances vary but all demand prayerful thought.

We might even view some of our homes as earthly houses of the Lord because he was so clearly at work in preparing them. They, too, become places where he is served, through outreach and hospitality. If he cares about the details and domiciles of this life, how much more does he care about what lies ahead.

Places of meeting

Traditionally, the more formal meeting place for most of God's people is, like Solomon's Temple, purpose-built. It can range from the lofty cathedral of a big city to simpler buildings elsewhere, but all act as gathering points for believers. A recent letter from South Africa tells how a local chief has given the villagers land and, although the people are very poor, they are determined to create a church building, using tree branches and flattened oil drums. In contrast, there are now so many parts of Europe where redundant churches reflect the general decline in attendance that there is a move to set up 'churches without walls' with more informal services open to all in local communities.

In many parts of the world, the persecuted church has had to go underground, perhaps meeting in different homes with frequent changes of venue as their numbers (and risks) increase. In 1991, a teenager from Albania, temporarily in Britain, attended the first church service of her life and was asked to outline her background. She told how her devout grandmother had told her that she could pray, even though at that time it was a punishable offence. She therefore whispered her prayers in the secrecy of her room and found that God answered them. This faithfulness put to shame and provoked repentance from the easygoing attitude to church attendance of at least one man present that day. Whether practised openly or covertly, and whether part of a congregation or not, the focus of our praise and worship is God the Father and Jesus Christ his Son, enabled by the Holy Spirit.

'Church' means God's own people

The church is not merely a building. When Jesus said that he would build his church 'on this rock', he was not pointing to a suitable building site but referring to the solid affirmation of faith in his deity just made by Peter.[2] The true church is the body of believers, commonly referred to as 'the church' in the book of Acts. As Paul said to the men of Athens, God no longer lives in temples made with hands.[3]

In fact, Paul taught that the body of each believer acts as a temple for the Holy Spirit. We might rarely think of ourselves as 'houses of the Lord', yet surely we should every day be 'places of worship'. Paul defined a spiritual act of worship as our response to God's mercy – the responsive offering of our bodies as living sacrifices, holy and pleasing to God, in return for the supreme and costly sacrifice made for us.[4] The worshippers he seeks are to worship him in spirit and in truth, and only he knows when this is happening.[5] In *The Purpose Driven Life*, Rick Warren points out that we have often reduced worship to an hour or so on Sunday morning – or even to a praise session within the service.[6] In reality, worship is intended to be a lifestyle, so the way we live our lives should give authenticity to our praise.

Such worship is not measured in decibels, but by dedicated discipleship. For this, our Lord holds the gauge, not our fellow believers. Having said that, personality no doubt plays a part in the way individuals choose to make music to the Lord, or to head for a particular style of congregational church service, whether this be quiet or exuberant, liturgical or informal. Yet God can surprise us out of our prejudices.

Trying to bring heaven down to earth

My own taste veers towards simplicity, but I once walked into a place far from simple and was moved to tears by the statement it was making. Thanks to a friend, I was one of a party taken on a tour of Austria's Melk Abbey, a young guide telling us its history and showing us some of its treasures. We had an impression of grey stone walls, lofty ceilings and high windows, obscuring the sunlit river view outside and contributing to the sense of austere living within. The only lighter touch was in the Marble Hall. It was decorated in a *trompe d'oeil* style that made the room look much higher than it really was, leaving us bemused and a little amused. It was at this point that our guide said she could take us no further. We were next to go to the chapel, but in silence, and she would leave it to make its own commentary. The only forewarning she gave was that whereas Gothic architecture attempted to take men's eyes heavenwards, the baroque artists sought to bring a little bit of heaven down to earth.

That is what we walked into. It was like entering a golden bowl, everything from its decorative cherubs to the holy table itself shining and shimmering in one equal light. I was stopped in my tracks, overcome by the unexpected impact and, for once in my life, caught the baroque vision.

Taking those on earth to heaven

If an earthly house of God can have that effect, what will it be like to see the heavenly headquarters unveiled? Certainly, it would be beyond David's imagination! There we shall no longer need a temple building, for we shall be directly in the presence of the God we have worshipped here.[7] We need to move beyond the Old Testament record for more light about this and, in the book named after his revelation, John indicated the impact on him of the heavenly glories, mysterious scene after scene bedazzling him defying description. We shall think of these again later but, after seeing the chapel at Melk, I can imagine in a tiny, earthbound way how completely overwhelmed John must have felt to be given a glimpse into the mysteries of the hereafter.

Is death the end?

It is a strange fact that a secular, materialistic society produces an ever increasing number of books to do with the spirit world, witchcraft or near-death experiences. People still seek help from faith healers before and from spiritists after the loss of a loved one, even when they would formerly have said, 'We're not religious'.

As recorded in 1 Samuel, when afraid for his life King Saul resorted to a risky consultation with a witch, despite both of them knowing that such practices had been expressly forbidden by God.[8] The woman reluctantly conjured up the prophet Samuel who, together with foretelling Saul's death and David's succession, underlined how seriously God takes disobedience, and how dangerous it was (and still is) to dabble in the occult. At the same time Samuel protested about having been disturbed. His death had evidently not been the end of him, but where had he been – purgatory or paradise, heaven or hell? Without that interruption would he otherwise have been there 'for ever'? The best place to start our search for answers is with the words of Jesus, the great David's greatest son.

What did Jesus say about the options ahead of us?

Possibly the best known of all Jesus' sayings specifically mentions that there is a way to avoid destruction:

> For God so loved *the world that he gave his one and only Son,*
> *that whoever believes in him shall not perish but have eternal*
> *life. For God did not send his Son into the world to condemn*
> *the world, but to save the world through him.*
> (*John 3:16-17*, my emphasis)

Love bids us welcome – and *such* love.

The Son referred to is, of course, the Good Shepherd who laid down his life for his sheep. It is not his will that any should perish and he promises eternal life (through spiritual rebirth) to all who have come to know and trust him as 'my Shepherd'. Jesus did not set up an earthly kingdom, but repeatedly referred to 'the kingdom of God', telling Nicodemus that entry to this kingdom was when 'the Spirit gives birth to spirit'. The new birth brings eternal, that is to say immortal life.[9] He often spoke of this gift of life eternal, telling them, 'The Spirit gives life',[10] not just awaiting us in a far off future but revitalising life now.

Eternal life

As a young child I sometimes tried to work out what eternity must be like (David's 'for ever') 'going on and on and on', and made myself dizzy in the process. In his last recorded prayer, Jesus clarified the concept by defining eternal life as to 'know you, the only true God, and Jesus Christ, whom you have sent'.[11] This puts us back into the familiar arena of getting to know someone with the assurance that this special relationship will never ever end. Jesus had already told his disciples that knowledge of God would eventually be mediated through his Spirit.[12] He assured them that if they remained in him, connected as branches are to a vine, he would remain in them, his Spirit acting like the flow of sap to a branch, ensuring life and fruitfulness. A disconnected, lifeless and fruitless branch would have to be disposed of in the equivalent of a garden bonfire.[13]

Just before he was betrayed in the Garden of Gethsemane, recognising that he was about to leave the world to go to his Father, Jesus prayed, 'Father, I want those you have given me to be with me where I am, and to see my glory'.[14] His earlier references to heaven had usually been linked to his (and our) Father's being there.[15] The implication must be that he wanted to see his own there too. As the dying Stephen indicated, he will be there to receive us as we emerge from the final valley.[16]

The alternative to life is death

Here comes the hard part. As well as his reference to dead branches, Jesus spoke plainly about the condemnation awaiting those who do not believe but, instead of being attracted to him as the light of the world, react with hatred because his light would show up their dark deeds.[17] His way might be narrow but it leads to life, whereas the more popular broad road leads to destruction.[18] He describes destruction as something we can choose to avoid, any personal cost involved in that choice being better than the alternative. For travellers on the broad road, this would be to 'be thrown into hell', where, with vivid imagery he said, 'their worm does not die, and the fire is not quenched'.[19] Here he is quoting from Isaiah, where God is speaking of the disposal of 'the dead bodies of those who rebelled against me'. Corpses are insensate but Isaiah describes the irreversible destruction of their remains as a warning to others.[20] Jesus would return as the judge, to decide whose choices would end so miserably or who could join him in his glory.[21] How much better to follow the Shepherd, whatever the cost, and know life to the full and forever starting now.[22]

Where do we go from here?

Very little of Jesus' teaching mentions what we can expect immediately after death. He once described a supposed conversation across a fixed gulf between a certain rich man as he suffered in 'hell' (or Hades) and Abraham, with the erstwhile beggar Lazarus safely by his side. Despite the sufferer's pleas for relief, no closer contact was possible. As this story followed Jesus' unpalatable message to the Pharisees that they could not serve God and money, the rich man's fate would be an awful warning about their own dangerous attitude as, like him, they regularly walked past the desperate need on their doorstep.[23] They would know their Talmud and that being 'in Abraham's bosom' or 'paradise' referred to the resting place of the righteous dead, and that Hades was the presumed destination of the wicked dead, both the good and the bad awaiting the final judgment.

Whether or not Jesus intended to support these teachings of the Talmud, the main point of the story is that the road taken in life governs what will happen in death. Jesus repeatedly gave solemn warnings that there are two categories of the dead: those made spiritually alive by the Spirit of God who will continue to enjoy eternal life, and those without him who cannot experience this. They were spiritually dead when physically alive, so in death have no bridge into eternal life – but their story will not end there. The all-knowing God who 'remembers that we are dust' in life[24] will have no problem when the approaching day of judgment requires the dust to be located, resurrected and refashioned. Some will reign with him whilst others await his final judgment.[25]

Looking ahead with Jesus

Before his death, Jesus spoke comfortingly to his disciples about going to his Father's home to prepare a place for them, adding that he would come back and take them there to be with him. To follow him as the way, to practise his truth and to receive from him his life would ensure that outcome.[26] He did not know exactly when his return would be, but it would be sudden. He accordingly warned his listeners to be ready, or face separation from him.[27] He would come 'in his Father's glory with his angels', and this would be a time for him to reward each person 'according to what he has done'– eternal life would be given to those who had denied the self-life in order to follow him, but those who had only pursued ambition and gain would thereby have forfeited the survival of the soul.[28] He also hinted to his disciples of an eventual 'renewal of all things' when he would reign and give them new responsibilities and authority.[29]

In his last teaching before his arrest, Jesus promised his disciples the gift of his Spirit who would help them to understand what he had been telling them. At the time, this must have seemed as mysterious to them as perhaps it still does to many today.[30] The coming of the Holy Spirit at Pentecost (after Jesus' death, resurrection and ascension) did indeed revitalise, inspire and activate them, as the book of their subsequent acts so clearly illustrates. We are told that the same Spirit can be ours as we accept God's offer of eternal life through faith in and response to the sacrifice of the Son in our place. He acts as a deposit, our guarantee that we will know this new life beyond death, and for ever.[31] It is his indwelling that makes us the temples of the Lord during our earthly lives.

To read again Jesus' Parable of the Vine in this context is a reminder that the purpose of being 'in Christ' is for his life in us to bear much fruit and so to glorify his Father.[32] This is part of the Spirit's work in our lives, and the first of those fruits should be the same self-giving love as was shown by Jesus.[33]

Guaranteed to last for ever

Any reader still unsure of what it means to be spiritually alive is invited to make a thoughtful consideration of the seventh and eighth chapters of Romans. There Paul offers a deeper exploration of this vital subject than this brief outline can encompass.

He reminds us that many experience a futile attempt to go it alone and become self-condemning, often despairing, in the process. Rescue comes from Jesus Christ our Lord as we gratefully hand over to him life and its problems.[34] Romans chapter eight begins with the wonderful affirmation that there is now *no* condemnation for those who have so entrusted themselves to him. John Wesley's diary tells how he found it life-changing to read and respond to this liberating statement, with the assurance that the Spirit is given to indwell those who believe and receive and are now counted as being 'in Christ Jesus'.[35]

Belonging to Christ and having the life of his Spirit go together [36] and this will last beyond death, for the Spirit 'will give life to your mortal bodies'. This might refer to our final resurrection, but also applies to the newness of life we can experience here and now.[37] We are freed from the slavery of wrong-doing and fear of its consequences, but instead are assured that we can now call God our Father.[38] When we don't know how to pray to him, the Spirit helps and intercedes for us[39] just as Christ Jesus, raised to life by that same Spirit, always intercedes on our behalf.[40] There are repeated hints that we should not expect an easy life, but the Spirit will energise us to hold on in faith whatever happens. The guarantee of his presence is thus no insurance policy against an experience of life's problems, but it does act as an assurance policy in that, whatever happens, his sustaining love will never fail and glory awaits us.[41]

In all things God works for our good to make us, in the end, like Jesus and part of his family.[42] As was the case with him, all opposition will finally be defeated. Having given his own Son for us, God will graciously give to us all things we need as his children.[43] Whatever the varied forms of opposition, God is for us, so Romans chapter eight ends with the gloriously triumphant affirmation that there is nothing, *including death*, with the ability to separate us from the love of God that is in Christ Jesus our Lord.[44]

This chapter should also encourage us in our concern for our beautifully created world, currently 'groaning' in frustration (polluted, stripped of its forests, with species of flora and fauna already dying out). It too will be 'liberated from its bondage to decay',[45] to become the new heaven and earth that John's vision later goes on to describe.[46] The victorious, resurrected and ascended Christ will finally bring to fruition the loving plans of God for all that he has made.

Love never ends

We can be confident that this love, yearning to draw us to himself and restore us to his image, will go on and on for ever. Although we can choose to risk going our separate ways, despite his warnings, he will not spurn a prodigal's return even at the last moment. As an old couplet puts it:

> *Betwixt the saddle and the ground*
> *I mercy sought, and mercy found.*

Better though to invite him to take the reins earlier than that and to know the Spirit's guarantee that 'it is well with my soul', both now and for ever. How astonished David would have been to find that one of his descendants was going to achieve all this! We can imagine his amazed delight when at last he experiences the full, endless glory of the 'house of the Lord'.

1   1 Chronicles 17:1
2   Matthew 16:15-18
3   Acts 17:24
4   Romans 12:1
5   John 4:23,24
6   Warren R. *The Purpose Driven Life*. Grand Rapids, Michigan: Zondervan, 2002.
7   Revelation 21:22
8   1 Samuel 28:5-19
9   John 3:3-6
10 John 6:63
11 John 17:3
12 John 16:13-15
13 John 15:4-6
14 John 17:24
15 Matthew 6:1,9
16 Acts 7:56
17 John 3:19,20
18 Matthew 7:13,14
19 Mark 9:43-48
20 Isaiah 66:24
21 Matthew 25:31-46
22 John 10:10
23 Luke 16:13-15,19-31
24 Psalm 103:14
25 Revelation 20:5
26 John 14:1-6
27 Matthew 24:36-44
28 Matthew 16:24-27
29 Matthew 19:28
30 John 16:12-15
31 2 Corinthians 5:4,5
32 John 15:1-17
33 Galatians 5:22
34 Romans 7:21-25
35 Romans 8:1,2
36 Romans 8:9
37 Romans 8:10,11
38 Romans 8:12-16
39 Romans 8:26,27
40 Romans 8:34
41 Romans 8:18
42 Romans 8:28-30
43 Romans 8:31,32
44 Romans 8:31-39
45 Romans 8:21,22
46 Revelation 21:1-7

19

In the house of the Lord – for ever?

A small boy lay in his bed, sleepless and rigid with fear. His Sunday School teacher had told the children that everybody must die one day and then those who had ignored God's offer of salvation would burn for ever and ever in the fires of hell. The thought understandably terrified him, and any tentative response he had made to the love of the Shepherd was quenched. As he grew up, his retrospective indignation at her message and its traumatic effects left him doubtful of the very existence of a God who could hand out such dreadful punishment.

Death comes to all

Jesus loved children and spoke stern words to any who offended them or caused them to sin.[1] Our natural end is to die but those with any sensitivity at all must, like that little boy, shrink from the notion of hell to follow. We prefer to think that a merciful God will somehow arrange for us all to end up in the house of the Lord for ever. That is what he would prefer, too, and he has already made provision for it, to be rejected at our peril.

Any references in the Bible to destruction as a possible end to our story are far outweighed by loving invitations to find eternal life (such as that in John chapter 3, verse 16) not just in the hereafter, but here and now. We should therefore give some hard thought to the basis of our present lives and future hopes. There are difficult questions to be faced, although not all will be answered until we know as we are known.

Jesus gave greater emphasis in his teaching to people's eternal destiny than to what happens immediately after death. The traditional view of a rapid flight to heaven, possibly somewhere high in the sky or, in another direction, to purgatory, is not expressed in his teaching. Once out of our familiar time space reference points we are in unknown territory and must own at the outset that there are mysteries still hidden from us. Yet humans are innately curious and by nature exploratory. We also realise the recurrent necessity for seeing that what has become encrusted with tradition is sound at the centre, and concordant with the biblical evidence. Other godly minds, with the Spirit's guidance, have tried to look into this but, whilst still earthbound, can only have hazy vision.

Dualism or dynamism?

There are some who argue that the unity of body, mind and soul that constitute the person cannot be divided and so the soul, or spirit, can have no independent existence. To their minds, this would smack of the old Greek philosophy of dualism, also held by some early Christian sages who deemed the body to be the prison house of the soul, its liberation depending on deliverance from all bodily influences. To this end some of them sat on top of pillars in the desert for years, certainly to the detriment of their physique but less certainly to the advantage of their souls.

Proponents of a continuing body/soul unity refer to Paul's teaching in 1 Corinthians chapter 15. Although 'flesh and blood cannot inherit the kingdom of God', in the resurrection we shall still have bodies, though this time they will be immortal.[2,3]

Professor Donald MacKay, international neuroscientist and Bible believing Christian, expressed his views with his habitual clarity in the scientific terms of his chosen discipline. The conclusions of my old friend and mind stretcher deserve to be read in full in the chapter headed *Mechanism and Meaning* of his book *Human Science and Human Dignity*. He had detailed knowledge of the essential role of cerebral activity in maintaining the vitality of the whole person. From this he would have found it misleading to suggest that ('like an invisible pilot leaving the cockpit') the spirit, or soul, escapes when brain and body die. Yet as God is the giver of personal significance to each human being, he also affirmed that the biblical promise of an eternal relationship with God would be sealed, not broken, by death. 'If it is our Creator's will that we shall again have our being as conscious agents in his presence, the provision of an appropriate body will be up to him.'[4]

Between death and resurrection

More light about the interval between death and resurrection comes from Paul himself. We must recall that he had been given special insights from God[5] and was probably the man 'caught up to paradise' who had heard 'inexpressible things'. Even though he was not permitted to spell these out, they must have coloured his views.[6] Accordingly, in 2 Corinthians Paul compares a believer's death to striking camp. The spirit moves out of a collapsed tent (the body) to 'an eternal house in heaven'.[7] In other words, with this removal 'what is mortal may be swallowed up by life'.[8] This could still refer to bodily resurrection, especially as he goes on to say that it was for this we were made, and that God's gift of the Spirit is 'a deposit, guaranteeing what is to come'.[9]

Our relationship with God takes us out of the arena of scientific proof, but in faith we believe that his Spirit indwells our spirits during our time on earth, establishing the eternal relationship referred to by Donald MacKay. As Jesus said and Paul reiterates, the Spirit gives life.[10] As we are assured that eternal life starts now, there can surely be no disjunction when we leave our bodies and move out of time into eternity. We can trust that the Spirit of Jesus will take us safely across that invisible drawbridge as we pray, even ahead of the event, 'Lord Jesus, receive my spirit'.[11] We are assured of new resurrection bodies in God's time, but surely the mysterious interaction between his Spirit and our spirits cannot come to an abrupt halt when our present brains and bodies die.

Paul seems to confirm this by his confidence that he would prefer to be 'away from the body and at home with the Lord', but whether here or there 'we make it our goal to please him'.[12] Elsewhere the apostle often refers to a Christian's death as having 'fallen asleep'[13] and looks forward to his own death as 'gain', because he would then be 'with Christ, which is better by far'.[14] As well as the reluctant reappearance of Samuel, there are a few other hints in the Bible that there could be some kind of resting place before the wake up call that will signal Christ's return.[15]

Supremely suggestive that the soul, or spirit, can survive bodily death, the God who so wonderfully designed us said during his own incarnation, 'Do not be afraid of those who kill the body but cannot kill the soul;' although he then added, 'Rather, be afraid of the One who can destroy both soul and body in hell'.[16] As he died, Jesus prayed, 'Father, into your hands I commit my spirit', having first assured the dying, penitent thief that they would meet in paradise.[17] After his resurrection, he must have said something, picked up by Peter, about going and preaching 'to the spirits in prison', held there since Noah's day because of disobedience, but that bare statement is all the explanation we have.[18] Although it is of course true that the experience of our Lord Jesus was unique, the martyr Stephen prayed a similar prayer as he died, first having said, 'Look, I see heaven open and the Son of Man standing at the right hand of God'.[19]

When death comes our way, therefore, we can do no better than to use the same dying prayer of committal to the Father, in the confidence that both the immediate and final outcomes are, indeed, 'up to him'.

Looking further ahead

Dr Tom Wright, New Testament theologian and Bishop of Durham, properly shifts our focus by saying, '"Going to heaven when you die" is not held out in the New Testament as the main goal. The main goal is to be bodily raised into the transformed, glorious likeness of Christ...an event which has not yet happened'.[20] Dr Wright finds no biblical evidence for purgatory and, whilst acknowledging that Paul's talk of 'sleep' in the Lord allows for the prospect of an intermediary heaven or 'paradise', he dismisses the popular conception of heaven as a particular place located in the skies. Rather, he suggests that a veil normally present will be pulled away and what is normally invisible will become visible – as for the dying Stephen. Elisha's terrified servant also had his eyes opened to see the chariots of fire between them and the enemy.[21] Perhaps this is what John meant when he spoke of 'a door standing open in heaven', through which so much was subsequently revealed to him, all leading up to the glorious reign of Christ, the Lord.[22]

The resurrection of Christ and of our bodies

The idea of bodily resurrection is naturally foreign to our temporal minds, and as we consider it we need to ask for God's wisdom and not trust to human reasoning alone. Like small children, we find something so far outside our present experience hard to understand. Yet there are sound reasons for believing that Christ rose again from the dead. Frank Morrison began by intending to disprove the resurrection but as he studied the subject was persuaded otherwise. His book *Who moved the stone?* is a powerful protagonist for belief and remains a classic with repeated reprints since it was first published in 1930.[23] We need to remember that with God all things are possible, and ask his help in enlarging our mental and spiritual horizons. There was originally a remarkable answer to the heartfelt prayer, 'I do believe; help me overcome my unbelief!'[24] Both the prayer and its answer remain contemporary possibilities.

In his discussion of resurrection in 1 Corinthians, Paul says: '...if the dead are not raised, then Christ has not been raised either. And if Christ has not been raised, your faith is futile; you are still in your sins...If only for this life we have hope in Christ, we are to be pitied more than all men. But Christ has indeed been raised from the dead, the firstfruits of those who have fallen asleep. For since death came through a man, the resurrection of the dead comes also through a man. For as in Adam all die, so in Christ all will be made alive'.[25] Paul was not only wise in the ways of God but also highly intelligent, and as the whole chapter pursues his argument it will repay careful and prayerful reading.

He will come back

Jesus had promised his disciples that he would come again. Paul's insights convey a clear (if extraordinary) impression of this promised return as Christ Jesus our Lord makes a dramatic re-entry into our orbit, heralded by the voice of the archangel and the sound of a trumpet, conceivably the reveille for 'sleepers', the dead in Christ. They will be resurrected and go to meet him in the air, followed closely by the believers still living at the time.[26] In a flash, in the twinkling of an eye, those still living and indwelt by his Spirit will find themselves totally changed, imperishable and immortal, and death will be swallowed up in victory.[27]

Paul mentions the 'book of life' in one of his letters[28] and so does John, writing in his book of Revelation.[29] It is evidently a record kept by 'the Lamb', John's name for the resurrected Lamb of God, Christ himself. The life referred to is the eternal life promised to those who have put their trust in him, and so been made eligible to meet him on his return. Only those named in the book are saved from the fate of those not recorded there.

John's amazing revelation

After delivering messages to the churches, John described in his book the strange and amazing happenings he was privileged to see in heavenly places. In his incarnation, the Shepherd had identified himself with his flock in all but sin, and in his sacrifice offered himself in their place. Accordingly, in heaven John saw him represented as a slain Lamb, now alive again and at the centre of his throne. Yet the Lamb still continued to act as Shepherd as he led those who had come through their valleys of tribulation to living springs, the old fear of bubbling water gone and tears wiped dry.[30]

John also describes angels, trumpets, a war in heaven and an ejected dragon. The kaleidoscope of shifting scenes goes on with beasts and more angels, innumerable white-robed worshippers singing new songs, eventually leading up to the best ever *Hallelujah Chorus*, sounding like the roar of a great multitude and rushing waters and peals of thunder all at once, and heralding the triumphant entry of the King of kings and Lord of lords.

It is hard to distinguish the language of metaphor from what is intended literally, or to know whether we have a colourfully expressed but coherent account of future events.[31] Yet the overall message is clear: the enemy of souls and those loyal to him will finally be conquered for ever by the Lamb, despite all the evils they have orchestrated in the interval against God's creation and against all the people of his world, whether or not they are recorded in the book of life. Already there will have been rejoicing in heaven over the greatness of God and of the Lamb and finally, judgment passed and all evil banished, there will be a new heaven and new earth where a redeemed people will dwell, not just in the house of the Lord for ever, but in the city of our God.

In Revelation chapter 20, John gives what does read like a sequential account. We are told that Satan will be bound for the same 'thousand years' as Christ will reign with selected holy and blessed martyrs.[32] The beheading they had undergone because of their testimony still happens today in parts of the world where Christians are a despised minority. At the end of the thousand years will come Satan's release, resurgence and final destruction, to be followed by the general resurrection and, after that, the judgment.

Sadly we do not see that name listed in our records

The millennium following the arrival of the King and binding of Satan would have given opportunity for all to realise what life could be like under the peaceful rule of Christ. Referring to the Lord's evident reluctance to bring in both judgment and destruction, Peter commented that, 'With the Lord a day is like a thousand years',[33] and *vice versa*. The story of those centuries of delay, whether symbolic or substantial, indicates how he does not want anyone to perish, but everyone to come to repentance. Even so, it seems clear enough that those whose names are *not* recorded in the book of life will be amongst those resurrected to face the judgment of God.[34] (Whatever the implied distinction, they will have been given up from the sea, death and Hades.) Echoing Jesus' use of Isaiah's imagery about the disposal of enemy corpses,[35] they will follow death and Hades into 'the lake of fire'. John explains this less graphically as being 'the second death', reminding us of Paul's warning, 'For the wages of sin is death, but the gift of God is eternal life in Christ Jesus our Lord'.[36] How much better to accept the gift than to earn such wages.

We will all face that judgment seat, whether or not our names are recorded in the book of life. Paul warned that our deeds would be assessed and the dross consumed, although when the book is finally opened, those whose names are found there will have nothing else to fear.[37] Their penalty has already been paid by the Lamb in whom they have put their trust and whose book it is. For them, new vistas open up.

All things made new: future hope and present possibility

John's account of his revelation builds up to a grand climax as he describes the renewal Jesus had referred to – a glorious new heaven and earth.[38] The Lord God Almighty and the Lamb will do away with the need for any other temple,[39] for the days of sin, sacrifice and suffering are over. God is at last united with his people and the Lamb with the church, his 'bride', now shining and shimmering in the light of the glory of God. So will Jesus' Gethsemane prayer be fully answered, as at last his own do indeed see his glory. It gives fresh hope already to think that this polluted earth will at last be renewed too, and the glories of the new heaven made marvellously visible instead of being any longer veiled from our earthbound eyes.

What happens next will come as a glad surprise, but we are not told exactly what it will be. It has been aptly said that the Christmas carol describing our future state as being all in white and waiting around gives too limited a picture, and our loving Lord will have much more delightful employment prepared for us than that! The new heaven and earth will inspire wonderful new songs of praise, thanksgiving and worship, leaving far behind all our earthly attempts to make music to the Lord.

Yet it seems likely that there will be work to be done, for work can be worship too. What John identifies for us are two future roles: his servants will serve him, and they will reign with him for ever and ever.[40] The perfect balance we saw in our Lord and Shepherd, ruler and rest giver, King and foot washer, will be shared by those named in his book of life who also reign and serve. The metamorphosis into his image will at last be complete.

Our response

Writing this chapter has been rather like struggling to put together the pieces of a futuristic jigsaw, with a few key pieces still missing. Different Christians hold differing views and interpretations about the events as described in a scatter of relevant Scriptures, and it might all seem incredible, even weird, to the unaided rational mind.

Paul said as much when explaining and extolling the power of illumination by the Holy Spirit.[41] The biblical references cited are mostly taken from Jesus' own words, or those of people (including Paul) who had met him after his resurrection and been enlightened by his Spirit. Why disbelieve their evidence or the truths behind their imagery?

Despite some residual perplexities, reason and faith are not mutually exclusive. Perhaps we need to ask what other reason than self-giving goodness and mercy could explain why Jesus, Son of God, should come into our world to die. How was it that the frightened men who ran away and left him at his arrest or, like Paul, became so hostile to his followers, were later so dramatically changed after witnessing his resurrection and receiving his Spirit? Why should some of them have been ready to give their own lives (as some still do) rather than deny that their Lord, Jesus Christ, was and is the way, the truth and the resurrected life? It was because they had heard the Shepherd's voice, seen the evidence of his self-giving love, and witnessed the power of his resurrection and ascension, believing the promise of his return to reign for ever with his redeemed and resurrected people. Now, through his Spirit, they bore (and others now bear) the same fruit in their lives, epitomised by an overwhelming love for him, spilling over into the lives of others and filled with the hope of life everlasting.

Paul still speaks:

> *Therefore, I urge you, brothers, in view of God's mercy, to offer your bodies as living sacrifices, holy and pleasing to God – this is your spiritual act of worship. Do not conform any longer to the pattern of this world, but be transformed by the renewing of your mind. Then you will be able to test and approve what God's will is – his good, pleasing and perfect will.*
> (Romans 12:1,2)

In his quaint but powerful poem *Christ our Lord*, George Herbert is troubled by a sense of guilt and unworthiness that hold him back from faith and trust. Four centuries later, doubt might well head his list, but will still meet the same love. The poem begins:

> *Love bade me welcome; yet my soul drew back*
> *Guilty of dust and sin.*

Then it seems that Love personified spoke to his confessed condition, holding out scarred and welcoming hands:

> *'And know you not', says Love, 'Who bore the blame?'*
> *'My dear, then I will serve.'*
> *'You must sit down', says Love, 'and taste my meat.'*
> *So I did sit and eat.*
>
> (*George Herbert, 1593-1632*)

1   Matthew 18:6

2   1 Corinthians 15:50-54

3   Cressey MH. *The Illustrated Bible Dictionary, Part 1.* Leicester: Inter-Varsity Press, Leicester, 1980.

4   MacKay D. *Human Science and Human Dignity.* Illinois: Inter-Varsity Press, 1979.

5   Ephesians 3:1-3

6   2 Corinthians 12:4

7   2 Corinthians 5:1

8   2 Corinthians 5:4

9   2 Corinthians 5:5

10 John 6:63; Galatians 6:8

11 Acts 7:59

12 2 Corinthians 5:8,9

13 1 Corinthians 15:6,18,20; 1 Thessalonians 4:13,14

14 Philippians 1:21-23

15 Revelation 6:9-11

16 Matthew 10:28

17 Luke 23:43,46

18 1 Peter 3:18-20

19 Acts 7:56,59

20 Wright NT. *For all the saints.* London: SPCK, 2003; Wright NT. *New Heavens, New Earth.* Cambridge: Grove Books Ltd, 2006.

21 2 Kings 6:15-17

22 Revelation 4:1

23 Morrison F. *Who moved the stone?* Carlisle: Authentic Lifestyle, 2004 (original 1930).

24 Mark 9:24-29

25 1 Corinthians 15:14-22

26 1 Thessalonians 4:13-18

27 1 Corinthians 15:51-54

28 Philippians 4:3

29 Revelation 3:5, 13:8, 20:12,15

30 Revelation 7:17

31 Wilcock, M. *The Message of Revelation.* Leicester: Inter-Varsity Press, 1975.

32 Revelation 20:2

33 2 Peter 3:7-9

34 Revelation 20:12-15

35 Mark 9:48

36 Romans 6:23

37 1 Corinthians 3:10-15

38 Revelation 21:1-22:6

39 Revelation 21:22

40 Revelation 22:3,5

41 1 Corinthians 2:12-16

20

Love bids us welcome

As I sit down to write this chapter, the evening's news bulletin is still in my mind. A teenager is missing from home, presumed to be with a boy she met through an internet chatroom but did not otherwise know. Her distraught family has appeared on our screens, pleading for her to come home and '...get this sorted out. We want her to know that we still love her. We aren't angry or anything. We just want her back'. This viewer has been left thinking of the father of a missing son who ran to meet him as, in despair, he trudged home with a grovelling speech at the ready, only to be enveloped in loving arms and given a great welcome, a new wardrobe and a slap-up meal as his 'sorting out'. Unlike his preceding stories about a lost sheep and a lost coin, Jesus left this one to make its own point.[1] The love of the Father for his wayward children is a yearning love, longing to have them at his side. He is delighted when the prodigals return and welcomes them home, to be showered with blessings, not blame. In the light of the warnings in the last chapter, we have to ask if it is ever too late to repent.

In thinking about the awesome matters of eternal life and death, I am reminded again that we are born in the image of our triune, inter-related God, and to that image he wants to restore us. Whatever else is implied, as a Trinity he knows the dynamism and strength of an intertwined relationship, but at Calvary also knew the agony of separation. In a modest way we see something of this imagery reflected when new babies and their parents enjoy face-to-face interaction. The relationship grows through its reciprocity and the child grows with it, but there is proportionate anguish when the bonds tear apart for whatever reason – an anguish known to all who have loved and lost.

Broken relationships cause serious damage

As with the rejected infants I have seen in Africa, India and Eastern Europe, growth ceased as love died and young hearts were broken. In 1991, half the abandoned children I saw on one such ward in an Albanian hospital simply faded away and were expected to die within a year. Offers of food and shelter were inadequate substitutes for personal love, and depression fatally lowered resistance to prevalent infections.

Reverse that situation in the spiritual realm and, instead of rejected infants, think of people who deliberately and persistently reject the possibility of a relationship with God. By ignoring his invitation to accept the gift of eternal life they must bring a fresh pang to his loving heart. Yet they damage themselves still more. They are like cherished children who turn against those who have lavished love on them, never again to communicate or visit and ignoring all loving messages from home. So it is with spiritual dropouts for, without a change of heart, their alienation becomes a self-inflicted death sentence.

Spiritual malnutrition and its consequences

With no fear of God in them – no searching for him or response to his Spirit, no gratitude for his costly plan of salvation, no interest in the evidence of his Word and deriding the testimony of his people – those who deliberately turn their backs on him develop dangerous malnutrition of the spirit. Without appetite for all things good they hunger instead for any alternative and are kept well supplied by the enemy of souls whose goal is to ensnare and ruin them. The bias to sin present in us all remains unchecked in them.

Frequently referred to as 'wicked' in the psalms, extreme examples of such people are those who specialise in doing evils of all kinds with no regard for those they hurt physically, psychologically or spiritually. We read of them in our newspapers and missionary magazines and hear of their doings from asylum seekers and bereaved families. We need name no names but could all quickly think of some especially notorious and unrepentant characters. The image of God in such people must fail to thrive as his love is kept at bay. Instead of the total metamorphosis he intended, their wizened spirits fade right away and, like those abandoned infants, are doomed to die. Lacking a creative relationship with God, they have unwittingly fallen into a destructive relationship with their worst enemy. The Bible is rich in picture language, the metaphor of the Good Shepherd being an obvious example, yet the images have a clear enough application. However vividly or metaphorically expressed, the implication is that, in whatever way destruction finally comes, it has at source been self-induced, through persistently making wrong and loveless choices.[2] In his book *The Great Divorce*[3] CS Lewis comments:

> There are only two kinds of people in the end: those who say to God, "Thy will be done," and those to whom God says, "Thy will be done". All that are in Hell choose it. Without that self-choice there could be no Hell'. He adds 'A damned soul is nearly nothing; it is shrunk, shut up in itself. Good beats upon the damned incessantly as sound waves beat upon the ears of the deaf, but they cannot receive it. Their fists are clenched, their teeth are clenched and their eyes fast shut. First they will not, in the end they cannot open their hands for gifts or their mouths for food or their eyes to see'.

What a dreadful picture of *rigor mortis* on the way, when the option is the free gift of everlasting life.

As we soberly reflected in the last chapter, judgment goes against any whose names are not found recorded in the book of life. Their imminent death and destruction will be an even deadlier fate than that of the abandoned babies, because it follows their deliberate rejection of love and not love's deliberate withdrawal from them.

Intransigence brings its own end

Even from the judgment seat, the unstoppable love of God must still yearn to draw the exiles home – for his love endures for ever. Our all-wise Lord is not willing that any should perish but that all should come to repentance. Yet just as with some of those wizened, dying babies, the exiles from God meet love too late to give the response that could have saved them. It seems that many of those who have persistently hardened their hearts to God's overtures in life are likely to shrink and shrivel from the impact of his blazing love and searing holiness when they finally meet him, rebellious to the end, and pushing away the hand that would embrace and cleanse them.

We are revolted by the pictorial image of being thrown into an everlasting lake of fire, but the message conveyed could be that advanced spiritual malnutrition has finally caused loss of the divine image and, as with the vine's dead branches, its intended temple must be disposed of. Like the Sunday School teacher mentioned earlier who so earnestly 'put the fear of hell' into the little boy in her class, some take literally what we dare hope was meant as metaphor and can then come across as though they actually wish that awful judgment to fall on conscious evildoers. Those holding a less literal interpretation are sometimes accused of heresy because their preferred emphasis is on the eternal love of our just and holy God. Both parties can quote from Scripture to support their views. Right at the other end of the scale are those who attribute to God a serious lack of justice and teach universalism, suggesting that everybody will be all right in the end, whatever their previous lifestyle.

John Stott, whose evangelical stance and teaching is known worldwide, raised some evangelical hackles when he tentatively suggested that the traditional view of 'eternal, conscious torment' needed to be looked at afresh. Minds reflecting on the fate of the wicked should be 'open to the possibility that Scripture points in the direction of annihilation', although 'both sides are faced with difficult texts'. He is quoted in *John Stott: a global ministry*: 'I am disturbed by the excessive dogmatism of those who claim that only one view is biblical. I plead for greater humility of judgment. We evangelical people need to give one another liberty in areas where Scripture is not absolutely plain'.[4]

In this view Stott had some distinguished supporters, as shown in this comment from his old friend Professor FF Bruce (FFB) who was recognised by many as the greatest evangelical biblical scholar of his day: 'Annihilation is certainly an acceptable interpretation of the relevant New Testament passages...For myself I remain agnostic'. To this John Stott responded, 'My own position is similar'. FFB's letter went on to say, 'To consign to eternal conscious torment is surely incompatible with the revealed character of God. I'd *like* to be a universalist...but...Our Lord's teaching seems plain enough: there are some who persist irretrievably in impenitence, and refuse to the end the only salvation that is available for them'.

There would have been no need for the Shepherd to give his life for the sheep if they could simply choose to go their own way with impunity. Why, then, do so many still stray away from his paths?

Why do so many wander away from the Shepherd?

Deliberate wickedness is not something we witness every day, but we do hear frequent excuses given for disbelief, presented as reasons by people who thereby miss knowing the fullness of life that could be theirs. Sometimes thinking themselves too sophisticated for what they see as either beneath their attention or irrelevant to their lives, they are in more danger than they could imagine.

I'm just not interested

Some of the infants I saw in Uganda had been bereaved, either by the death of the mother or by being distanced from her – the traditional local method of weaning a breast fed baby. This bewildering separation often precipitated serious malnutrition and one of its striking hallmarks was apathy, a listless immobility without a gleam of interest in what was going on. Even if a mother reappeared, the empty eyes still stared vacantly or turned their gaze away in rejection when she approached. Very occasionally a child might rouse to push her away, or even hit her. There had already been too much pain to readily risk being hurt again.

Using the code name of Screwtape for the enemy of souls, CS Lewis has him say, 'The skill of our Tempters has never stood higher'.[5] Four decades later this could be heavily underlined. One of Screwtape's favourite strategies is to induce spiritual apathy, which in some ways is worse than open hostility, for the drift tends to be imperceptible.

If such apathy is challenged, stories sometimes emerge of past hurt that has nipped in the bud any emerging interest in spiritual development. As with the bereaved infants, expectations have been let down. Some feel that God himself has let them down and, hurt and bewildered, they have gone off him without ever hearing what they are missing, or being helped to give him their pain and find his comfort. Apathy is one of the hardest conditions to meet because it is so hard to dispel a habitual lack of interest.

I'm much too busy for that kind of thing

Some institutionalised children spend their days in fruitless activity, rocking to and fro or head banging. Those able to do so pursue visitors with various attention seeking devices. Anything is better than feeling so deprived.

Overactivity can mask the emptiness at the heart of many, mostly from secular societies, who have become preoccupied with both trivial and profit making pursuits. Idol worship is still with us, the terms pop idol and football idol being symptomatic of a materialistic culture with scant interest in turning to the one true God. Pursuit of money, sex and power are other distractions, often used to try and fill what has been called 'a God-shaped gap'. Those in poorer cultures are busy surviving, but many still find time for their gods.

A pendulum will swing unless the clock has stopped. Currently, at least in Britain, there is a detectable move away from 'religion' and instead 'spirituality' is coming into fashion. Some get caught up in a kind of spiritual merry-go-round without any encounter with the Holy Spirit of God, but this gives opportunities for those who know him to make the introduction. Yet Christians too can simply be too busy, even on worthy affairs, to make a quiet space to be spent nourishing the soul with God and his Word and discovering his priorities. We might argue that he is with us all the time, but all relationships will falter without nurture.

I'll do it my way
We occasionally hear of street children, fostered or adopted children, and even some still safely in the parental home, who have experienced those comforts but choose to run away, preferring their own hazardous freedom to the constraints of love. Too late, many discover that such freedom leads only to demoralising bondage.

Autonomy is another 'in word' today. There are those who, faced with Jesus' dying words, 'It is finished', simply cannot believe that there is nothing left for them to do towards their own salvation except to repent, give thanks and receive newness of life. Instead, they try to go it alone, only to find that they do not even reach their own standards. Autonomy means self-government, but this is folly: 'For the wisdom of this world is foolishness in God's sight',[6] especially when on offer is the very mind of Christ.[7] Better to be warned by Solomon, 'There is a way that seems right to a man, but in the end it leads to death'.[8] It can be frustrating to approach such people with the message of God's love in Jesus, the hope of life lived in the power of his Spirit now and a bright future ahead with him. This can simply evoke the response, 'That's just your opinion. I've got my own'.

Is there no hope?
It is notable that after a major natural or national disaster spiritual questions arise and church attendance suddenly increases. It seems that God sometimes uses such events to wake people up to their need for his protection and salvation. Instead, the majority tend to give only transient attention, or blame him for what was often, at source, man-made, and then return to pre-occupations that exclude him.[9] Happily some do meet him in their valley experiences and life is never the same again.[10]

Sometimes the process of spiritual decline is reversed before it is too late by something like Paul's Damascus Road experience, or simply by at last paying attention to the Word of God. We thank God that there are still such testimonies of spiritual reformation and restored growth. Those who receive and believe the message of John chapter 3, verse 16 will be given the right to become God's children, with the privilege of an assured inheritance and the freedom to call him Father.[11] At last they know that they were loved enough to die for, and are assured that his love will sustain them through the changing scenes of this life and into the joys beyond.

Even in the last valley of all there can be a revelation. A farmer friend, too busy for more church attendance than the celebration of Christian festivals, and not given to spiritual conversation, became comatose when dying of cancer. Suddenly he woke up looking astonished and said, 'It's so wonderful!' He brushed aside his wife's 'What is it, John?' Clearly he wanted to stay with the vision he was so much enjoying. Reflecting later on what this had meant to him and conveyed to her was a comfort to his widow.

What about those who die without having heard, or who have misheard?

I approach this hesitantly as the short answer is that we do not know, but that is to apply a sticking plaster to the pain in the mind experienced by those who grapple with two seemingly opposed concepts. This particular question vexes many thoughtful people as it arises from the tension between belief in a God of love, Creator of life, who is nevertheless said to be ready to send to eternal damnation some of his beloved but rebellious creatures. Having already considered that such a sentence is not his choice but that of those unbelieving rebels, the question remains: 'It is one thing for someone to have reviewed the evidence of God's love and rejected both it and him, but how can he banish those who have not had the opportunity to choose?'

In trying to think this through, I now recall the empty but searching eyes of abandoned infants, or of the older children I met in Russian orphanages who expressed their longing to be adopted into a family but could never arrange this for themselves. There must be many spiritual orphans in the world who know nothing of God's love but, conscious of the void within, seek for someone like him. Meanwhile they might try to follow the promptings of conscience, or make do with substitute gods, but still stay unsatisfied. What will happen when they finally meet him?

A year after my encounter with those dying Albanian infants with the desperately sad eyes I returned and was amazed to see some of the same children. They were now plump and smiling with arms outstretched to welcome a wonderful woman who had made it her daily mission to bring love and stimulation into their lives. This was not the love they had lost in earlier life but it had been transforming.

We might conjecture that, like those previously rejected undersized infants, and the few fortunate orphans who blossom when at last embraced by new love, so certain deprived and diminished but searching souls could discover (even at the judgment seat) that the Lamb of God *always* lives to intercede for them.[12]

In John's vision, he was still a Lamb 'looking as if it had been slain, standing in the centre of the throne'.[13] As at last they meet him and see those scars and he beams out his tender love upon them, we imagine how their deprived spirits could make a glad response as at last they come home to him and discover his Shepherd's heart. Mirroring the words of his brother James, we can be confident that he will not exercise judgment without mercy to anyone who has been merciful, for mercy triumphs over judgment.[14] Although we have no specific chapter and verse for the idea, it is surely not outrageous to think that, in his mercy, the Lamb might enrol new names in his great book, even at the last moment.

Our Lord and Shepherd is completely trustworthy

In his short letter, Jude warns believers against 'shepherds who only feed themselves', but have slipped in amongst the faithful. They sound thoroughly and perversely bad and in describing them he uses the word ungodly four times in one verse.[15] All the same, it sounds as though some of the weaker believers had fallen under their influence, and he gives a moving appeal to those who, through the aid of the Holy Spirit, the love of God and the mercy of our Lord Jesus Christ have the assurance of eternal life, so are fitted to reach out to the others. He tells them, 'Be merciful to those who doubt; snatch others from the fire and save them; to others show mercy mixed with fear....'[16] They were to hate the stains of sin but still reach out to rescue the sinner. Jude was probably another of our Lord's brothers, and behind these words we can detect the compassionate influence of our just and merciful Lord and Shepherd.

Whilst many cannot bear to think of a loving God's eternal and adverse judgment falling on anyone, others sadly quote biblical warnings that for some it must do so. The resolution of this tension must lie within Abraham's conclusion when troubled by the threat of destruction hanging over Sodom and Gomorrah: 'Will not the Judge of all the earth do right?'[17] Abraham still pleaded with God to spare those heading for destruction, and the mercy of God would doubtless have done so, but the story implies that only a few in those cities were righteous, indeed most were frankly unrighteous, so his judgment had to fall. In FFB's words, they were amongst those who 'persist irretrievably in impenitence', to their bitterest end.

Centuries later, when confronted with such intransigence even in the face of his clear teaching and miraculous healing, Jesus warned that this would be considered even more culpable on the day of judgment than the sins of Sodom and Gomorrah. To have heard and rejected is evidently worse than to have sinned without knowing better.[18] He also said that words spoken against him, the Son of Man, would be forgiven but not so the blasphemy against the Holy Spirit – in context, this had been to attribute his healing work to the chief of devils and, he said, unforgivable 'either in this age or in the age to come'.[19] Whether or not these passages give us a hint that some sins might be forgiven in the age to come and the final judgment tempered in surprising ways, our conjectures about any probable outcome must finally come to rest in the confidence that the Judge of all the earth, whilst longing to restore all broken relationships with himself, also holds the scales of justice and mercy in perfect balance. However fierce the debate between supporters of differing views, he alone knows which way those scales should rightly tip for each one due at last to stand before him.

What about now?

What is not so comfortable is that in the interval he has left those who do know him with a great commission, to go and teach all nations.[20] Our task is not simply made more urgent by uncertainty about their future in the life to come, but by wanting to share with them the joys of walking with the Shepherd throughout this life. Perhaps more would have left Sodom safely if Lot had more earnestly shared with them his knowledge of God. How can people believe in the one of whom they have not heard – and how can they hear unless someone goes to tell them?[21] Other sheep he has, not yet in his fold, so the Shepherd needs many who are already his own to become trustworthy under-shepherds to go and gather them in. If our lives winsomely but humbly convey the wonders of the Good Shepherd's self-giving love, we could be used to convince the doubtful, arouse the apathetic, arrest the overactive and refocus the independent. In the end, though, only he can save the lost, by the prompting of his Spirit; it is his love reaching out that bids them welcome, wherever in the wide world they might be and through whatever channel he can find to reach them.

To energise us in his service we can enjoy the effect of the Lord Jesus' resurrection in our everyday lives here and now. In *Living the resurrection* Eugene Peterson describes the early disciples' experiences with their resurrected Lord and how their friendships, work and even meals together took on new meaning in his presence.[22] As he is still present through his Spirit, we can celebrate his resurrection in similar ways in our lives today, at the same time seeking to share the good news of his eventually coming to reign over all he has made. We have the friendship and fellowship of others to encourage us as we begin to know what it is to be serving the victorious King of kings here, as a foretaste of life with him hereafter. Some official letters are marked OHMS, and we too should be marked as those On His Majesty's Service.

Looking ahead

I had just been writing this when the telephone rang and I heard a voice from the past. Many years ago I looked after a delightful trio of children whose Christian parents have kept in touch every year since. Now the oldest of the three has died. For years, she had bravely struggled with chronic ill health, loyally supported by her husband and family. They in turn had been much affected and blessed by her open reliance on God. As she faced her death, it was later found that Kathy had already been 'living the resurrection'. She had written out some of Paul's strong words of assurance, so applicable to her condition and clearly underpinning her (and our) confidence in Christ:

> *Therefore we do not lose heart. Though outwardly we are wasting away, yet inwardly we are being renewed day by day. For our light and momentary troubles are achieving for us an eternal glory that far outweighs them all. So we fix our eyes not on what is seen, but on what is unseen. For what is seen is temporary, but what is unseen is eternal.*
>
> *(2 Corinthians 4:16-18)*

Like Kathy, we are to be encouraged by the anticipation of living with Christ, both here and hereafter.[23] Until then, we have been given a life to live, with tasks and responsibilities to get on with here and now. To enable us in this, as we learned from Romans chapter eight, we have the same Spirit that raised Christ from the dead to live in us and transmit the power of his resurrection, even should we also share something of his sufferings.[24] Peter amplifies this by saying that with this divine power we are given all that is needed for life and godliness.[25]

Glimpses of glory

Meanwhile, we anticipate the day of his coming for us, whether via the valley of the shadow of death or more directly. As we wait, we are sometimes given glimpses of the hereafter when witnessing the death of a believer. Rationalists, with their earthbound minds, might offer scientific explanations for what they would prefer to call wishful thinking, or hallucination due to impaired metabolism, but to those involved and attuned there is a real sense of awe as they are sometimes (but not always) privileged by the Spirit to share in something very special. Whatever the physiological explanation, the marvel lies in the message being conveyed to and through the one who is moving on.

Some years ago I had in my care a dying child of only eight years old who indicated to her parents, just before she died, that she was having a glimpse into heaven. She had roused from semi-consciousness and said, 'Why didn't you hear them singing?' Then her gaze fixed and an ecstatic smile illuminated her pale face. 'What are you seeing, Rachel?' they asked. She replied, 'Jesus!' A few minutes later, with an amazing surge of energy, she climbed out of bed to hug each parent in turn – then immediately died, her father's arms about her. Although naturally grief stricken, her parents believed that their little girl had indicated to them how the Good Shepherd was waiting to welcome her home.

Some time before, Rachel had speculated about what gift to offer Jesus when she met him, and had decided that a hug was probably something that he would really, really like. Her parents found great comfort in believing that she had not passed from life to death but from death into life – and from their arms to his. Later, the Bible on her coffin lay open at Isaiah 40, verse 11: 'He gathers the lambs in his arms and carries them close to his heart'.

> *"No eye has seen, no ear has heard, no mind has conceived what God has prepared for those who love him" – but God has revealed it to us by his Spirit.(1 Corinthians 2:9-10)*

What was it Jesus said? 'You also must be ready, because the Son of Man will come at an hour when you do not expect him.'[26]

1   Luke 15:21-24

2   Matthew 25:41-46

3   Martindale W, Root J (eds). *The quotable Lewis.* Wheaton, Illinois: Tyndale House Publishers Inc, 1989; Lewis CS. *The Great Divorce.* New York: MacMillan, 1946.

4   Dudley-Smith T. *John Stott: a global ministry.* Leicester: Inter-Varsity Press, 2001.

5   Lewis CS. *Screwtape proposes a toast and other pieces.* London and Glasgow: Fontana Books, 1965.

6   1 Corinthians 3:19

7   1 Corinthians 2:16

8   Proverbs 14:12

9   Jeremiah 6:16-19

10 Revelation 11:13

11 2 Corinthians 6:18; Galatians 4:4-7

12 Hebrews 7:25

13 Revelation 5:6

14 James 2:13

15 Jude 15

16 Jude 22,23

17 Genesis 18:23-33

18 Matthew 10:11-15, 11:20-24

19 Matthew 12:24-32

20 Matthew 28:19,20

21 Romans 10:14

22 Peterson EH. *Living the resurrection.* Colorado Springs: Navpress, 2006.

23 1 Thessalonians 5:10,11

24 Philippians 3:10

25 2 Peter 1:3

26 Luke 12:40

21

I know my sheep and my sheep know me John 10:14

As I reach this final chapter, it is 70 years almost to the day since a small girl solemnly knelt by her bed, her mother beside her, and they gave her life into the Good Shepherd's keeping. He already knew where and how he would lead her, but for years she was taught to read his Word and carried along the right paths by his under-shepherds, primarily her parents, rather than being conscious of any other leading or even of being led. Lambs enjoy green pastures and still waters without thinking too hard about how they got there. It would be years before she grew in understanding and grasped the personal implications of honouring her Shepherd as Lord and being indwelt by his Spirit, but she was always grateful for those early years when, like Timothy, she was taught to learn the Holy Scriptures.[1] Christian parents please note!

In years to come, the Shepherd would lead her to take care of other young children, and her own experience was the assurance (sometimes to be shared with grieving parents) that there are none too young to be brought to Jesus, neither can any stray beyond his care. No valley is ever too shadowed for his light to penetrate and he longs to lead and bless, always and for ever.

For her, the twenty-third psalm has never become commonplace and, looking back down the years, it now seems that the path of life has followed each verse in turn, with the Shepherd patiently and faithfully showing the way. There have been many times of undoubted leading (often seen more clearly in retrospect) yet times of hesitancy and doubt, too, especially when travelling through some of life's gloomier valleys. The darkest of these was traversed in Uganda, a country and people she would learn to love, but of course at first it was not in any way like home and the wrench was painful. Her address for some months was Cottage 23, Kitante Valley – imagine her wry surprise to find that, when translated, this meant 'The valley of the slaughtering of the cattle!'

That was an experience of verse four, later to bear fruit in a deeper understanding of loss and the varied reactions to bereavement as well as much else, but at the time the Shepherd provided the comfort of Christian friends and offered hope that verse five would follow – and so, in due course, it did. Time and events have only served to enlarge her exploration of the psalm's inner meaning.

Theory is now backed by practical experience, leading to ever growing gratitude for the never failing goodness and mercy of her Lord, to be relied on for the rest of the days that remain until she moves with him, out of time and on to eternity.

The Lord is indeed her Shepherd. Is he yours? Then come follow.

May the God of peace, who through the blood of the eternal covenant brought back from the dead our Lord Jesus, that great Shepherd of the sheep, equip you with everything good for doing his will, and may he work in us what is pleasing to him, through Jesus Christ, to whom be glory for ever and ever. Amen.

(Hebrews 13:20-21)

And when the Chief Shepherd appears, you will receive the crown of glory that will never fade away. (1 Peter 5:4)

I   2 Timothy 3:15